BE THE DEAL

BE THE DEAL

WILLIAM GLADSTONE

Waterside Productions

Be the Deal

Printed in the United States of America

2019

ISBN-13: 978-1-943625-36-9 POD edition
ISBN-13: 978-1-941768-92-1 ebook edition

Waterside Productions

2055 Oxford Ave
Cardiff, CA 92007
www.waterside.com

To Gayle Gladstone, my inspiration, guide, and fearless partner in love and life.

ACKNOWLEDGMENTS

I would like to acknowledge my father Milton H. Gladstone who was my mentor in book publishing, my mother Selma Gladstone who loved books and inspired me to pursue writing my own books, and my brother Thomas Gladstone who made life fun and showed me that fun is integral to success in business. I am also thankful to the hundreds of authors I have represented, the wonderful publishing professionals at dozens of book publishing companies with whom I have collaborated, and the diligent employees at Waterside Productions who have allowed me to focus on creative deal making and inspiring others to create books and products that contribute to a better world for everyone.

PREFACE

A Note for the 2019 Revised Edition of *Be the Deal*

It is quite rare for a book to be written, edited and published by the same person. Given the unique nature of this book it is also appropriate.

Be the Deal was originally published in 1998 by ToExcel, a startup company that was introducing the concept of print on demand to book publishing. I wrote the book in less than ten days and the book was never edited, copyedited or proofed. The reason I wrote the book was to demonstrate the readiness of print on demand publication technology for the potential investor at that moment which was Barnes and Noble. Based on the business plan and sample book, Barnes and Noble invested twenty-eight million dollars in ToExcel's parent company Kaleidoscope Software Inc. A year later, Warberg Pincus invested an additional forty million dollars. Through mergers, To Excel became part of Author House, which was sold to Random House Penguin for more than one hundred million dollars. Random House has since divested Author House, and I am not sure if Author House remains profitable, but it is ironic that a book entitled *Be the Deal* sealed the deal for an innovative enterprise in the world of book publishing.

For many years, I have been contacted by law firms and other businesses that have told me that they have made *Be the Deal* mandatory reading for their new hires. I was pleased that this was the case, but was too busy to go back and reread *Be the Deal* myself. I had remembered that I had written the book while on holiday in Kauai and that because we needed a finished book so quickly, I focused on lessons I had learned throughout my own business career. *Be the Deal* is essentially my business biography. Miraculously, it is also a wonderful handbook on how to create your own luck in business and how to be a successful negotiator. I was surprised and pleased when reading to see how timeless and relevant the advice still is.

I have made almost no changes to the original edition. With so much time having elapsed, I have the rare opportunity of sufficient distance from my own writing to serve as my own editor to correct some of the minor typos and redundancies that slipped into the original publication. I greatly enjoyed the process of revisiting the secrets to my own business success and am sure that you will as well.

I strongly suggest that you share *Be the Deal* with the young people in your world, especially those who have an entrepreneurial spirit and a sense of adventure. I have led an extraordinary life and learned so much on my journey. Fortune favors the brave, and *Be the Deal* is a handbook on how to be both brave and fortunate in every aspect of life.

May all go well in every aspect of your life.

TABLE OF CONTENTS

CHAPTER 1

INTRODUCTION

*B*E THE DEAL: *Seven Insights That Will Help You Create Your Own Good Luck in Business* is a book about deal making. It is also a book about creating your own good luck. It is also the autobiography of an unorthodox but highly successful literary agent and dealmaker.

In writing this book, I had hoped to reduce my unique business wisdom to a series of maxims and formulas of success that could be shared with others. To some extent, this has been achieved, but for many it will be exasperating as well, for the maxims often contradict themselves and the formula is a nonformula. And yet, bear with the process because the maxims and nonformulaic formula work, and at least parts of each can be applied by anyone to almost any situation in order to improve their own deal making and their capacity to experience good luck in their business life.

The contradictions and paradoxes that you will find in reading the following business biography are almost the essence of what I want you to learn. I remember the profound sense of awe I felt as an adolescent when I discovered that the secret to life is that there is no secret. That is actually a very liberating realization and one that is more important to keep in mind today than ever before.

We are entering a chaotic period of transition in business and in all aspects of life on this planet as we approach the twenty-first century. It will no longer be business as usual, and *BE THE DEAL* may well become one of the first true lampposts to the new way of doing business. I have tried to give this philosophy of the new paradigm a name and the best I could come up with is the term "nonlinear success." I am not really sure what I mean by this phrase by itself, but it has something to do with the quantum unexpected leaps and synchronicities that have governed much of my personal and business life.

I have been told that the term "nonlinear" is somewhat obtuse so I have decided to use it only when it seems to clarify rather than obfuscate a point I wish to make. I forewarn you to be alert to this term, and if you find it useful (as I do), so much the better.

The title for the book came from one of my clients who was fascinated with my total absorption in deal making. I believe that he was thinking of the Bill Murray character in *Caddyshack* who used to meditate on "being the ball" in order to achieve golf perfection. I have focused on being the deal in order to achieve deal-making perfection.

Since the entire book is about how to be the deal, I won't go into too much detail here, but suffice it to say that being the deal involves putting the deal you are negotiating above all else and actually getting inside the structure, purpose, and long-term potential of a deal so that you move from representing short-term formulaic interests to representing the living, creative energy that a great deal can become.

My background is book publishing, the movie industry, and mergers and acquisitions, with some expertise relating to the communications and computer industries. Most of the sample deals will be in those areas, but the basic principles should apply to any industry. In most cases, my deals have involved buyers and sellers just like any other industry deals, but there is usually a creative talent that I represent and a business-money side that I do the deal with. I have always maintained that, as an intellectual property broker, I sell dreams. Often there is nothing tangible in the deals that I am representing. Yet, in many cases, millions of dollars are invested on the basis of intangibles alone. In this regard these deals are different from real estate, oil, and manufacturing deals, and yet deep down perhaps the differences are more apparent than real.

I can assure you that you will learn about deal making and creating good luck for yourself in reading these stories and the analysis attached to each. I also hope that you will be amused by these stories. They are true stories and in many cases are extremely outrageous. I am not suggesting that everyone try to pattern their work life after my own quirky approach, but I do suggest that some awareness of the principles of deal making that have worked for me will greatly enhance your own approach to deals and business.

My credentials for giving you advice include having personally closed over two thousand deals and having created a literary agency that has closed over five thousand deals. I am proud that out of all these deals we have never had a single lawsuit and have only had a handful of situations where lawyers were even consulted. I am also pleased that over 90 percent of all deals negotiated by my agency have resulted in profits for all parties to the negotiations, not just the clients that I have represented.

At my most active, I personally closed 299 book deals in a single year. That may well be a world record, for it represents better than a deal a day. My system has worked well for me, generating tens of millions of dollars in personal income for myself, hundreds of millions for my clients, and billions of dollars for the book publishers with whom we have entered contracts. Along the way, I have bumped shoulders with some of the top people in the computer and publishing fields ranging from Peter Norton, John Sculley, John Doerr, and Bill Gates, to Bennett Cerf, Nat Wartels, Alberto Vitale, and Pat McGovern.

Since I never really set out to do any of this when I started, I very much identify with Robert Cringley's description of the accidental millionaires of Silicon Valley. It helps to be bright, but it helps even more to be lucky. I have been extraordinarily lucky throughout my life, and whether just dumb luck or smart luck, know that luck is not really arbitrary at all. This book will provide you with some examples and let you draw your own conclusions. As Steve Jobs used to say, "The Journey is the Reward." May you enjoy the journey that you will find in this book and have an opportunity to apply it to your own life.

Chapter 2

Abe's Oddysee and the Saga of OddWorld

A Case Study in How to Be the Deal

"Hello, is William Gladstone available?"

"No, I'm sorry; he is not. Who is calling?"

"This is Harry Rubin, president of GT Interactive. I need to speak to him immediately."

"I'm sorry; he went on a trek into the jungle with a kapuna."

"Did he bring his cell phone?"

"No, he didn't."

"WHAT? He didn't bring his cell phone?"

"I don't think that cell phones work in the Napali."

"But he should have taken his cell phone. This is an emergency. We need to talk to him right away. This deal has serious problems. Let him know that this deal may be dead."

"He won't be back until tomorrow."

"Well, have him call me as soon as he gets back."

"OK."

"And let him know that he has to take his cell phone. This is a delicate deal. We need him available at all times."

"I'll tell him."

"Thank you, and make sure he calls as soon as you hear from him."

"I will."

"Good-bye."

Thus began the saga of the negotiations to sell OddWorld to GT Interactive. As a case history in *How to Be the Deal*, much can be learned from this saga, which by accounts of all involved was one of the most difficult, contorted, and complicated deals in their collective professional lives. My own involvement in the deal came about more by accident than design.

Every career must reach different stages if it is to be dynamic. At a certain point in the development of Waterside Productions, I became immune to the highs of the ever-increasing profits and successes of book agenting alone. I took a more active position in the computer book industry and started to become involved in mergers and acquisitions of entire companies. I had some early success, which addicted me, like a gambler, to this as a fun and profitable pursuit. Only later, after being cheated out of commissions, after spending an inordinate amount of time with some less than stellar corporate citizens, did I learn to take a step back and restrict myself to what actually was the fun part of these deals, at least for me: serving as finder and negotiator rather than full-service broker.

One semi-unsuccessful merger led me to being appointed to the Board of Directors of CPTV, a startup conceived by Gary Vickers and backed by his longtime associates, Gary and Kim Magness of Colorado. This was an appealing group on the surface, since Kim and Gary Magness were the sons of Robert Magness, the largest shareholder in the then high-flying John Malone Company, TCI (this was the year of the attempted merger with Baby Bell, which generated a short-term paper net worth for Robert Magness in excess of six billion dollars).

As presented to me, CPTV was to be the beginning of a very large media conglomerate that would eventually leverage the Magness vote at TCI into some attractive and lucrative future media opportunities related to games and other entertainment products. I eagerly joined the board and waited for the next step. Well, there were a number of next steps, but they all seemed to be missteps.

After losing almost three million dollars of the initial eight million dollars raised through the original public offering, the head of CPTV, Gary Vickers, finally found some top-of-the-line talent with an interesting idea. This talent was Sherry McKenna and Loren Lanning. Sherry and Loren had superior credentials in their past but had never created a video-type game on their own. They had a great concept and were looking for backing. Gary Vickers understood the value of their concept and idea and offered to put up two million dollars to create the first of what would be five games. As a board member, I was aware of the risk of backing relatively unknown talent to this degree, but their credentials were strong and overall it looked as though CPTV could afford this level of risk.

About nine months into the project we received news that OddWorld as we had named our subsidiary was far behind schedule and would require at least another million dollars to complete the game. This was troubling since it now put in jeopardy whether or not CPTV would be a strong enough financial player to market the game once released. Having now had some experience through agenting in the process of due diligence on creative projects, I went ahead and commissioned the top game expert in the Waterside camp, Rusel DeMaria, and was told, "I can't guarantee you a best seller, but the game has some breakthrough qualities and will certainly be a major release if the parts come together and are executed as planned at this stage." Well that was enough for me and with that report to guide us, the board, in our wisdom, allocated another million dollars toward completing the project.

At this time, it was apparent to all that CPTV either needed to find some additional funding of its own or seek a marketing partner to take over the publishing and marketing of OddWorld's game, then called *Soulstorm* but eventually released as *Abe's Oddysee*. Both courses of action were pursued simultaneously. It was at this point that the relationship between CPTV's chairman Gary Vickers and OddWorld heads Loren Lanning and Sherry McKenna began to deteriorate. It is not my purpose here to place blame or provide analysis of the nature of the disputes, but they were severe. Since in the end everyone has avoided lawsuits to date, I do not wish to provide enough information to reinstate the lawsuits that are still set to go among the principals. Suffice it to say that it was worse than war.

Some of the issues related to the stability of the engine that was to pull all the game elements together and allow smooth game play. At different points in time the viability of the engine was either asserted as sound or faulty by all the major players. Memos started to circulate from Sherry McKenna directly to board members challenging assertions made by Mr. Vickers. Mr. Vickers discounted any word coming from OddWorld and the status quo among the principals was that no one was to be trusted on any point no matter how small.

The contract Mr. Vickers had negotiated with OddWorld enabled CPTV to take control of the OddWorld board in certain default situations. Based on lateness and cost overruns, this was done and I found myself the only volunteer to serve on the OddWorld board as well as the CPTV board. Part of the reason there were no volunteers was that the liabilities for serving on the OddWorld board seemed high and there was zero compensation offered to serve. I chose to volunteer for two primary reasons. One was authentically altruistic—I believed in the game we were financing and that there had to be a way to bring some rationality to the situation so that the investment we had made could be recouped. The second reason was probably more related to ego and my own sense that without resolving this situation it would end up being a disaster to have been involved with CPTV at all and there would be no way to leverage the success of this game into future successes. No matter how big the deal, I am always thinking about the next deal the current big deal could lead to and I was again in this mindset.

When Mr. Vickers convened the first two or three OddWorld board meetings, Ms. McKenna and Mr. Lanning chose not to attend and instead hired a top-notch attorney in LA, formerly personal legal counsel to Mr. Lou Wasserman himself, and this top-notch attorney advised Ms. McKenna and Mr. Lanning not to recognize this new board at all. In the middle of the battling boards, an initial offer had come in from GT Interactive to purchase the rights to publish the game for an advance of several million dollars with a marketing budget in excess of one million dollars. This was a good start and an offer that was not to be dismissed out of hand. There was also strong interest from Activision and other major players.

Ms. McKenna saw the problems on a going-forward basis with any buyer and adroitly sidestepped the chain of command and was able to interest GT president Harry Rubin in making an offer to purchase CPTV's 50 percent interest in OddWorld for a cool seven million dollars. This seemed quite attractive to CPTV board members, as it would get us back to even in terms of our capitalization and avoid the costly search for additional capital to launch *Soulstorm* ourselves.

But between an initial offer and a closed deal there can be many slips and the animosity among the parties certainly aggravated the negotiations. In the first place, Vickers was threatening to sue McKenna and Lanning for noncompliance with their initial agreement. Under the terms of that agreement CPTV could take 100 percent control and ownership of OddWorld. This seemingly clever negotiation at the time of the agreement was too clever by half. It created such an insupportable burden that there was no room for compromise but only an explosion when things went awry as they often do in the creation of an entertainment product. McKenna and Lanning could not admit to any wrongdoing whatsoever and followed sound advice in contesting the proposed action of CPTV. They were also advised to simply declare bankruptcy as a way of protecting their intellectual property assets and thwarting the loss of two years of labor. To add to the complications, both OddWorld and CPTV were running out of cash and the doors at OddWorld could not remain open unless another $500,000 of CPTV money was contributed to the game effort.

The GT interest had surfaced in April and it was now late June. What could be done? There was no way for CPTV to provide this money without going back to Gary and Kim Magness and Mr. Vickers personally to provide this additional working capital.

Rightly or wrongly, the three had to extort a pound of flesh for this highly risky additional $500,000. The pound of flesh was that they would be in first position and McKenna and Lanning would again be in the street even if the first level of action against them were decided in their favor by the courts. Of course, the wise attorney for Sherry and Loren advised again not to sign this preposterous note.

It was at this stage that I became involved. I had by now developed some rapport with Sherry though only having met her once. I eventually came to trust Sherry and believe in her abilities, but it was a process of several months because she had been so badly stigmatized by the surface dealings she had had through Mr. Vickers and CPTV. In any event, the final negotiations for this note were handled by me and it was messy since lawyers kept having to call lawyers to be authorized to speak with me, since there are all kinds of laws governing client-attorney privilege and what attorneys can and cannot do in relation to outside adversarial parties once legal actions have been filed. Somehow, I prevailed upon Sherry that she had to trust that the CPTV board had some rationality and decency, that the onerous clauses in this note would not be enforced, and that by signing the note she had a chance, slim though it might be, to complete her life's dream's first stage by completing this game. I explained that is was game over if she didn't sign it, because even though she might have a solution through bankruptcy, the game industry moves too fast and by the time bankruptcy had worked its way out and the new team had assembled, technology would have passed this game by. It would just be too late to receive any recognition for her work, much less the remaining minuscule possibility that new financing could be found to complete the game at some future date.

Even though Sherry didn't know me well, she heeded my pragmatic advice—of course it's not fair, of course it's not right or even decent, but it is the only viable future step you have—and, showing great courage, signed the document that bought both CPTV and OddWorld another ninety days of run time with which to negotiate the final contract with GT. As it turned out with back debts included it really only bought another seventy-five days, and, as it ended up, we needed every one of them.

At this point rancor had developed between GT's Harry Rubin and the Magness brothers and Gary Vickers. I attribute much of this rancor to differing worldviews since the Magnesses and Vickers represented the real estate and Colorado mentality, McKenna and Lanning the Hollywood view, and Mr. Rubin the Harvard Business School/New York view. I have been told that I am just being kind, but it is my kindness throughout this process that probably saved the day. I would venture that had I had a truly proper background in mergers and acquisitions, I would have realized early on that this negotiation would never come off and that we would all end up in bankruptcy court with no assets to argue over. But I didn't know all that and even though I knew enough to know this was going to be a very bumpy ride, I saw a worthwhile goal, not to mention worthwhile game, and decided to plunge forward.

I received a call from Harry Rubin requesting that I be point person for all further negotiations. He no longer trusted Vickers or Magness and did not want to deal directly with them. Vickers and Magness did not like the idea of me being point person, but since they controlled the purse strings, they felt that I was manageable and would probably help rather than hurt their goals.

An initial letter of intent was negotiated with much back and forth and several days of the deal being dead. Finally, when the letter of intent was worked out, we realized we had an even bigger problem. As a public company, CPTV would need to get shareholder approval on the deal once signed. This could take an additional ninety days. At the present OddWorld burn rate, this could require another $625,000. Where would this money come from? GT was prepared to put up this money but only upon receiving a personal guarantee from Gary and Kim Magness to reimburse the entire amount should shareholder approval not be provided. Since I argued that the odds of this were relatively infinitesimal, Kim and Gary reluctantly agreed. This took place in July; we had only the letter-of-intent agreement which specified what would be agreed to but actually didn't yet agree to anything, so all eighteen subagreements that would eventually form the base agreement had to be drafted by attorneys, debated by opposing attorneys, re-debated by the drafting attorneys, again debated, etc., until eventually there might be a document that perhaps all parties at the last minute would or would not sign.

The next seventy-five days were horrible. I received calls morning, noon, and night regarding arcane legal points that could totally change the way the deal was being negotiated. Every time we solved one problem, it created a score of others. The problems ranged from the tax status of previous investments and the accounting practices relating to intellectual property and technology to the viability of reps and warrants with each party and OddWorld and CPTV claiming exemptions based on complications from the other. Other problems included going forward budgets, financial responsibility for the leases that were accompanied by pending lawsuits from other parties, and other minutia of the deal too exquisite to burden anyone not part of the industry.

In the end, I kept coming up for air and assuring all parties that this deal was not dead and that we could find solutions to each and every objection. The level of distrust between all parties exacerbated all negotiations and made it a virtual minefield. At one point, CPTV required access to the accounting records from OddWorld and OddWorld required additional cash from CPTV. Since there was a major dispute over the acceptable and appropriate use of past funds, CPTV decided to dole out money as it deemed appropriate, not as OddWorld felt appropriate. This created a truly hellish atmosphere. I was stuck negotiating payment in exchange for the release of information necessary to close the deal. It was a true Mexican standoff but one in which both parties seemed more intent on destroying each other than surviving. I would go from a conversation with Sherry in which she would indicate that Mr. Vickers belonged in jail and that she had evidence she could use to incarcerate him to hearing in slightly stronger language the same opinion from Mr. Vickers regarding Ms. McKenna.

It would have been easy and perhaps rational in such circumstances to deal with these emotions and become enraged in the process, but I did not. I would listen and allow what needed to be said to be said and then return to the action points, if any, that might move things along. As we made progress toward the finish line, a few unexpected problems arose. Mr. Magness did not feel that the industry standard of a holdback for the intellectual reps and warrants was a valid negotiating point. He accused Mr. Rubin and GT of bad faith negotiating because originally they had said it would be a clean deal, seven million and no complications. Mr. Magness felt the $700,000 escrow holdback was a complication. GT thought it was straightforward business with no complications since this was the industry standard. (In fact, 15 percent or a $1,050,000 would have been industry standard in this instance). I was blamed as the messenger of these bad tidings, but in the end, Mr. Magness agreed to the holdback for some other concessions. It was an awkward negotiation because without the personal guarantee from the Magness brothers there could be no deal. Even if the CPTV Board of Directors voted for approval, Mr. Magness had the ultimate veto, so I had to find a deal that all parties—GT, McKenna and Lanning, G. Vickers and Magness, and CPTV—could approve. I almost short-circuited the success by not realizing at a certain point a fifth constituency entered the negotiations—the lawyers themselves. The esteemed law firm of Mr. Wasserman's former counsel had racked up a bill of close to $250,000. This bill had to be paid to close the deal and there was a huge dispute since CPTV felt that some of those expenses were expenses created by McKenna and Lanning to contest the actions of CPTV earlier in the year for their own interests, not those of OddWorld. An ingenious negotiation developed in which GT ended up paying half the bill in exchange for royalty relief from Lanning and McKenna from points that they retained to actual game sales. But then this issue bit us again in the final days because the esteemed attorney felt that he could not give a fairness opinion, without which the deal could not close because of the potential liability his firm would suffer if the deal did not close due to shareholder disapproval of the deal. Another ingenious solution was worked out to this end that required calling the head of the esteemed attorney's law firm and threatening that the deal would crater over this issue and working out a solution that generated 90 percent of the fee paid without liability.

In the final days of the negotiations, Harry Rubin had to fly off to London so the timing of calls became even more difficult. We were down to the nitty-gritty but there were still approximately $350,000 worth of assets in dispute relating to the value of used equipment, liabilities on leases, etc. CPTV wanted to hold firm on these issues, but the deal was crumbling on GT's side. Harry flew back from London to a Board of Director's meeting and was told that GT could not give another penny, that the market was changing, and that GT now thought they were overpaying for the asset. With so much work in the deal Harry did not want to lose the property and asked me to fly to New York along with all the lawyers and all the principals to save the deal and make sure we had closure by Friday since his board would not extend the time for negotiations beyond that date. This was a Wednesday and it was clear that time was now critical. In addition, OddWorld was again out of money and had been unable to make its last payroll and was going to have to close the doors unless another chunk of money came by that Friday. CPTV was also now broke and the largess of Magness had been tapped so it really was down to the eleventh hour.

I checked the plane schedules from Kauai where I was living and realized that it was impossible to get to New York until late Thursday night. This would give us at most twelve hours to wrap up negotiations—not enough time. Instead, I suggested that all other parties convene in New York for the closing and that I would handle last minute negotiations from Kauai. From Wednesday night on until early Friday morning New York time, I did not sleep. I had calls throughout the day and night from all parties and attorneys. There were money issues on the table, but these could be resolved. What seemed impossible to resolve was the conflict over who would accept the reps and warrants on the property itself. Without these reps and warrants, there could be no deal. In the end, it was decided to put statements into escrow with the understanding that such statements of reps and warrants were null and void if the deal did not close because of lack of shareholder approval. This was extremely clever because it allowed both sides to maintain that the other was lying if they had to duke it out in bankruptcy court but allowed GT to have sufficient reps and warrants to close the deal if bankruptcy were avoided.

As we came down to a final dozen points, it was agreed that McKenna and Lanning would be in one room of the lawyer's offices, Vickers and his attorneys in another with Harry Rubin and the GT lawyers, and that I would conduct the meeting via phone from Kauai. I burned through two cell phones, but in the end agreement was reached and signed off by all parties. To bring the parties to New York for those final negotiations had been extremely unlikely. The positions of McKenna and Vickers were such that it seemed hopeless. I ended up calling the private counsel of Mr. Vickers and telling him that the deal was dead and that unless he could get Mr. Vickers to that meeting there was no point in contemplating future negotiations. He at first did not believe me (I was calling him at home at 11 P.M. Wednesday night his time), but when he finally realized I was not being dramatic but factual, he hopped on a plane and flew to New York after making a key phone call to Ms. McKenna. His call reassured her to the extent that she too flew in, despite having been in New York in vain the previous week, since those earlier negotiations blew up without the closure that had been promised.

Was this deal truly a miracle? Perhaps. In the eyes of the world at large this was one small negotiation over a game and nothing more. To the people involved it was closer to life and death. Was there a simple formula that I followed to keep this deal alive? Again, yes and no. I contradicted myself a number of times and was forced to be patient and subdued, only to have to be aggressive and even alarmist. How did I know what to do when? The truth is I didn't. In each moment I listened and assimilated new information as it became available and acted accordingly. I remained open minded and flexible and trusted in a higher wisdom than my own to guide my actions. I allowed my actual interaction with Sherry McKenna to determine my ultimate view of her veracity rather than previous extremely damaging knowledge (tapes were made of many conversations throughout these negotiations by a third party that reflected badly on almost everyone). I did several unconventional things that helped.

(1) I did not change any of my behavior patterns for the benefit of this negotiation. I never got on a plane and flew to New York despite being asked to several times. The main reason I did not was because my children were visiting and I was not going to eat into any more of their time than these negotiations already were. I remember one time I had arranged to take a hike with a native guide into the Napali coast of Kauai and that no cell phones would function there. I went anyway, despite the protests from GT and others.

(2) I realized from the beginning that this was not going to be easy and that no single moment until the end would be the end; that no single setback would be the setback until the deal was at least twice dead. As a result, I never attached overmuch importance to any short-term setbacks.

(3) I was unambiguous about the benefits of closing this negotiation for all parties. It was absolutely clear to me at all times that a closed negotiation was a win-win-win and that anything short of it would be disaster. The game market was moving too quickly and there was no second-best alternative to this deal. I did not allow distractions brought to me by other CPTV directors relating to continuing interest from Activision and others in being a white knight to deter me from focusing exclusively on the GT negotiations as the only possible solution. This is where getting the tools of the trade really matter. I had enough background in fast-moving intellectual property negotiations to realize that time was of the essence. There was this point in time and no other.

(4) I tried not to judge anyone. There were near-slanderous comments made about almost everyone during this process. I paid little attention and did not attempt to gather any information on any topic that was not essential to the negotiations at hand. I did not care who had done what to whom or what might seem "just." I focused on the power of the parties, the possible outcomes for each, and the right action for each. I became the deal not allowing the egos of the players to ever intrude on the necessity of the deal itself, as well as its integrity. The game, the creative effort of dozens of people, the financial faith of shareholders in a public company; these were my concerns and only these. The deal itself was more important than the interests of any single group, and by maintaining this perspective, I was able to deflect numerous assaults against the deal.

(5) I connected with everyone involved in the deal from the perspective of their highest and best. I did not wallow in the fear issues that all held but tried to connect with what was the best outcome for each individual throughout the negotiations. I genuinely saw the positive contributions of everyone and acknowledged them freely. I sympathized with those in weak positions but remained firm with what I knew had to happen and concessions that had to be made to get the deal done.

(6) I OVERRULED ATTORNEYS. In several instances, not just the case cited earlier in this tale, I counseled clients not to follow their attorney's advice. I did not try to vilify the attorneys or even disagree with the legal advice. I simply explained the consequences of following that advice and the possible upside of ignoring it.

(7) I TRUSTED THE ATTORNEYS. I trusted the attorneys and listened to them. I followed their arguments and understood the seriousness of the risks I was recommending their clients take. When possible, I shared additional information with attorneys so that they could formulate elegant solutions.

(8) I trusted everyone involved in the negotiations and tried to learn from them all. I did not try to take center stage; I tried to remain a secondary player—available to help but not directing the negotiations until the very end when called upon by all parties to do so. I allowed each party to dictate strategy even when I thought the strategy would fail until such time as there was no time.

(9) I kept doing other deals. Somewhat mitigated, it was true, and nothing requiring too much creativity or emotion, but I kept my other business interests in sight and did not allow this particular negotiation to throw off the normally balanced and positive atmosphere of the majority of the negotiations with which I am involved. By doing this, I prevented a negative vortex of energy relating to the GT deal from being created and overwhelming my own sense of balance, purpose, and being in the flow. I am sure that the success of other negotiations during this period had a positive, if subtle, impact on the OddWorld deal.

(10) I did not ignore linear rules and wisdom. I was not naive about the stakes and perspectives of the parties involved. I did not bring a Pollyanna attitude that everything will work out in the end to the negotiations. I believed this to be ultimately true, but I also realized that each party was extremely aggressive in pursuing their own self-interests and that every possible means would be used by every party to obtain their goals whether legal tools, negotiating ploys, or hardcore pressure tactics. I did not divorce myself from my awareness of how business ordinarily operates.

(11) I did not limit myself to linear processes. If I had limited myself to the tried and true wisdom governing negotiations, this deal would not have happened. That knowledge was a starting point for me, not an ending point. I believed from the beginning that against all odds the transaction would close. I believed that it was meant to close and that somehow nothing could stop it from closing. I had my faith in this

belief severely tested and ultimately had to detach myself from the result.

(12) I detached myself from the end result. Not entirely, but enough. I would have been sorely disappointed and saddened had this deal not closed. I would have felt a personal sense of defeat and loss. Nonetheless, I was not a principal to the negotiations but a bystander. I had been roped in from necessity, not by design. I had my own business to run and no significant economic interest either up or down in the outcome (total fees received after the successful negotiation were well less than five percent of my average annual compensation). Because of this I was able to stay objective, and despite putting my all into the effort, was willing to chalk it up as a learning experience had I failed. This ability to retain such equanimity under such severe trauma is perhaps the essence of the nonlinear approach to business. It seems absurd to put so much effort into trying to create an end result and to then walk away from the events as though they did not matter. And yet it must be so. To some extent, man or woman can make the effort and final results reside with a higher power. An awareness and humility of this fact perhaps allows God to smile on our endeavors and reward us. In any event, this had a happy ending with the game going on to become a major best seller and no doubt leading to other games, all of which seem a step above the normal blood and guts games put out by other companies. There was something magical in the product and the concept that deserved to be published, and so it was.

CHAPTER 3

THE BIG BANG

The Birth of Arco Publishing and
the Heritage of My Father

Even before I was born, I was destined to run a book publishing company. In fact, part of the motivation for my conception was to do just that. That moment occurred in the spring of 1949, but our story really begins much earlier with the creation of the book publishing company I was destined to run, ARCO PUBLISHING. Arco Publishing was founded in 1936 by Milton H. Gladstone, the man destined to be my father. A little background music first.

Herbert M. Gladstone was born in Brooklyn, New York, in 1915 to Max and Rose Gladstone, Hungarian immigrants from Budapest who purportedly left Hungry to escape from numerous debts associated with the high living style enjoyed by Max. Max's family was rather distinguished in Budapest, with one of his uncles being responsible for the city's entire educational system. The life style was affluent for the times but not nearly to the level to which my paternal grandfather Max aspired. Max was a great bon vivant, extremely generous, and a snappy dresser to boot. Unfortunately, he was ingenious but not significantly successful as an entrepreneur and constantly found himself with expenses far exceeding income (a sure formula for financial ruin, as we know from Charles Dickens' novel *David Copperfield*).

By the time Herbert was born, Max was still an unsuccessful entrepreneur, but his debtors were now American and not Hungarian. According to my mother, who had a less than stellar relationship with Max and Rose and who therefore might be subject to some hyperbole, the Gladstones moved almost annually to keep one step ahead of their creditors. They imbued in Milton not only a gypsy-like quality of instability but also a tremendous entrepreneurial streak based on his own survival needs that, unlike his father's, led to financial stability. Milton did it with flair similar to Sergeant Bilko (of television fame) and kept alive his father's sense of grandiose generosity, limitless potential, and seat-of-the-pants pragmatism in his business dealings from earliest days on.

Just a few of Milton's early triumphs include creating his own miniature golf course while living in the Bronx at the age of twelve and his unique revenue plan while on scholarship at City College of New York to provide nude models for male would-be artists to draw for college credit. This was in the 1930s when access to female nudes was something difficult for the average young boy to obtain. Zero Mostel, the famous actor was a partner in this venture. The enterprise produced significant positive cash flow until it was shut down by the college authorities on the basis that the art school instructor, Zero Mostel, though talented, was not properly credentialed to run an art school on college property.

Milton was a brilliant scientist and received the highest award in chemistry that City College bestowed. He was a student of the chemist Ury, who was one of the most prominent chemists in the world at that time. Based on his aptitude and achievement as a student, upon graduation from City College Milton was awarded one of only two jobs offered by Union Carbide as a working research chemist in New York City. Milton seemed headed toward a relatively stable life as a professional chemist, but life is what happens while we are busy making other plans. All of sudden, KABOOM!!! An explosion in the chemistry lab totally altered Milton's life.

The explosion left Milton partially deaf in one ear and required a six-month paid leave of absence from the lab. Milt spent the six months going to ballgames, dating young curvaceous women, and generally attending to the necessities of life, such as renewing his driver's license. The renewal process at that time required taking a written examination similar to the examinations still given today in most states. This being New York City and automobiles becoming ever more popular with the masses, the lines for renewing licenses were long indeed. After waiting nearly half an hour to make an appointment, Milt got to the head of the line only to be informed that the sample booklets containing the test questions for review had run out and that he would have to come back the next day if he wanted to obtain one. Well, Milt came back the next day, but unfortunately (or fortunately as it turned out in the long run), there was a shortage of booklets again. Well, Milt (ever enterprising) tried to buy one of the booklets from the man six people ahead of him in the line who had received the last booklet before that day's supply had run out. "I'll give you a dollar for that booklet," offered Milt. "No way," replied the stranger. "I need it myself."

Undaunted, Milt proceeded to make a similar offer to the twenty or so people milling about who had been fortunate enough to receive a copy before the supply ran out. Most turned him down, but finally there was one who for two dollars, a not insignificant sum in the spring of 1936, said OK. Well, Milt took the booklet home, studied for the exam, came back the next week, and passed his driver's test. But this was not the end of the story. Milt was an observant young man and while taking the written examination he noticed two things. First, a fair number of people failed the exam and were told that they would have to come back and take it again. Second, he noticed that again there was a long line to receive the study booklets and that again the supply ran out early in the day, leaving a number of distraught would-be licensee renewal candidates without assistance of any kind to prepare for a driver examination test with questions completely unfamiliar to the general population.

Milt put these two observations together and came to the conclusion that there would be a market for these question booklets so inadequately supplied by the state. Before investing more time and energy in fulfilling this potential demand, Milt visited the nine other licensing offices located throughout the five boroughs of New York and observed that in each office the booklets were in short supply, with some not receiving any at all for weeks at a time.

In thinking through the opportunity, Milt decided that just printing up the booklets would probably suffice but that he might make an even more astute refinement: He would provide the correct answers as well, since having taken the examination himself he now knew the right answers from the wrong ones. Milt's next task was to find a secretary to type up the booklets with the answers filled in (they were multiple choice tests, so this was just a matter of typing an x next to the correct answer). He was friends with a young woman who was working at the Abraham Rosenfeld Company as a secretary typist, and he arranged for her to retype and mimeograph a hundred copies of the booklet with answers. The next day, he presented himself at the license bureau of Manhattan around two o'clock in the afternoon and, sure enough, again they ran out of the booklets. Within minutes, Milt had sold his entire stock at a dollar a copy to the would-be test takers.

Milt repeated this process for the next several days. He now had a profit of several hundred dollars and realized he needed to increase production. The secretary was doing the mimeographing for Milton at night after the Abraham Rosenfeld Company closed for the day. Abraham and Rosenfeld were commodity brokers, so this was not a problem except that as Milton increased his production from one hundred copies a night to five hundred, he needed to provide enough paper and ink on a daily basis to meet the larger production run, and therefore needed storage space in the office as well. With money in his pocket, Milt proposed that he lease a quarter of the office from Mr. Abraham and Mr. Rosenfeld for fifty dollars a month. This seemed a reasonable fee to the two traders, and soon Milt was able to churn out a thousand mimeographed booklets a night. This was somewhat more than any single licensing bureau would require no matter how inadequate the state-provided booklets might be, so Milt got some of his former college friends who were still in school to recruit other students to take a hundred or so booklets to each of the other licensing centers throughout New York City on the basis that they would receive a quarter for every copy they sold at a dollar a piece. This arrangement continued for several months with Milt accumulating a profit of several thousand dollars a week, which was very good money in 1936 and far more than he could ever hope to make as a chemist.

In 1936, unemployment was still high as the country struggled to come out of the Depression. Military service at that time was not so much of a requirement as a privilege and a solution to unemployment. The level of pay and opportunity for continuing education in the Army was determined by performance on the Armed Forces entrance examinations. A low score would remove any chance of being admitted and a high score would not only get you admitted, it would be noted on the application as a sign that upon completion of basic training, testing would be available to qualify candidates for officer consideration and additional training opportunities.

Getting into the Army was considered very desirable by most of the general population struggling to survive economically. Milt had a college friend who became a recruiting sergeant and who explained all this to Milt over a couple of beers as Milt was sharing the largess of his success as the author and publisher of the only driver's education test prep booklet with answers. Milt inquired if he could get hold of a copy of the examination being provided to recruits, and his friend saw no reason why not since, just like the driver's manual, it was a public domain document produced at taxpayer's expense. The examination wasn't too tough, covering mostly basic math and English, and Milt was able fill in the answers pretty easily and take the copy back to his corner of the Abraham and Rosenfeld office where he mimeographed a few hundred copies to test the market. The next day he went to sell the motor vehicle booklets with a hundred "Practice for the Armed Forces Tests" booklets under his arm as well. The Armed Forces booklets sold even faster than the motor vehicle booklets. Soon Milt had his college crew of part-time salespeople hawking the "Practice for the Armed Forces" booklets in front of every recruiting station in the five boroughs of Manhattan. He was selling thousands of these booklets a week and was well on his way to making his first million dollars within just a few months of that Union Carbide KABOOM. When the disability payments for the six months of paid leave ran out, he barely noticed. He also declined the invitation to return to the Union Carbide lab.

With the money rolling in, the test booklets selling like hot cakes, and the increased activity in his comer of Abraham and Rosenfeld's office, Milt realized that he now had a real business and that he would need to incorporate. He also needed more space to accommodate his ever-increasing production of test prep booklets, as well as the increasing need for some administration over his salespeople and cash flow. As luck would have it, the fortunes of Mr. Abraham and Rosenfeld were going in the opposite direction, most particularly for Mr. Rosenfeld who expired shortly after agreeing to rent a corner of his office to Mr. Gladstone. Mr. Abraham realized that as a single trader he no longer needed such a big office, and he approached Milt with the idea that Milt should take over the lease altogether now that he seemed to have such a thriving business. This was soon agreed to and shortly after Mr. Abraham removed his remaining belongings (leaving the extra desks, chairs, and office equipment at a very fair price to Mr. Gladstone and his new enterprise), the landlord of the Park Avenue building where all this was occurring was duly informed of the change of tenants and sent his handyman to remove The Abraham Rosenfeld Company name from the door.

Milt happened to be in the office when he heard the scraping of the gold paint being removed from the door to the office. He came out and the "The" had already been removed, leaving an ornate

Abraham
Rosenfeld
Co. Inc.

in gold letters with the capitals ARC beautifully crafted in the style used by sign makers back in the 1920s and earlier when the letters had first been painted. Milt thought it would be a pity to have this workmanship removed, so he told the handyman to leave the capitals and the "Co. Inc." and only remove the other letters. This left A.R.Co, Inc., and not wanting the added expense of adding words to the capital letters, Milt decided to name his company ARCO, and so incorporated his fledging publishing enterprise. His company soon expanded into other test prep areas, concentrating almost exclusively on New York City civil service examinations in the beginning so that his transportation and distribution costs on his first books were minimal and directly under his watchful eye. Still in his twenties, Milt was a self-made millionaire from the test prep books before being drafted into the armed forces himself in 1942, but that is another story that we will save for chapter four.

In analyzing the birth of Arco, there are lessons to be learned. By the way, since my dad died some time ago I have not had the opportunity to verify all the details, which is somewhat disappointing as I know his own retelling of the tale would have included several embellishments worthy of recounting, particularly the small details of what he was thinking as the story evolved. The point is, however, that this is really a creation myth as much as it is a factual story, and as a myth, it served to set the tone for my own business life. In some version or other this story was told to friends around the dinner table on different occasions and served as the grand creation myth for the Gladstone family, since Arco was the economic fountain from which all blessings flowed throughout my childhood.

Lessons to Be Learned:

The way the Arco creation myth was presented and interpreted to us as children, the following points were made either explicitly or implicitly:

(1) No event in and of itself is totally good or bad. The explosion in the lab certainly was not a "good" event, yet it led to fortuitous results that would not have been pursued otherwise.

(2) There was a depression going on when Arco was created, but that wider economic depression did not impact the financial

fortunes of starting a business such as Arco. To some extent, the dire economic opportunities for the population at large increased the likelihood of economic gain for a company offering booklets that could lead to employment. The lesson was, "Do not be overly concerned about wider economic trends or the fortunes of others, but focus on your micro-world and the opportunities present therein."

(3) Inquiring minds want to know. My dad might have just reacted with disgust each time the motor vehicle center ran out of booklets. Instead, he made inquiries to see whether or not this was just his misfortune or a wider phenomenon.

(4) Test your concept on a small, safe scale. Milt did not run out, raise a lot of money, create a business plan, and start producing thousands of booklets overnight for the perceived need of the public to buy motor vehicle test prep books. Instead, he carefully stuck his toe in the water. He used a casual friendship with a secretary to print a few dozen booklets at no expense. Knowing my dad, he probably "borrowed" the paper from Rosenfeld and Abraham for the first run of booklets.

(5) Do the initial marketing yourself. For the first week, Milt did all the selling himself. In this way he was able to determine what was involved with attracting buyers and soliciting them in a way that would not conflict with the goals of the motor vehicle employees themselves (the employees were actually grateful when Dad showed up with the booklets since this satisfied the otherwise irate renewal applicants upset with the lack of state provided booklets). Dad eventually determined that he needed to sell the booklets on the street corner since sales in the buildings themselves were prohibited. This led to alliances with the newsstands in front of some of the offices and the expansion of newsstands to other sites upon Milt's advice and promise of steady business.

(6) Enjoy and share your success. It was through treating friends and sharing the success story with buddies such as

the recruiting sergeant that Dad became aware of the even greater opportunity of selling the Armed Forces test prep guides.

(7) Do not be too attached to past success or past efforts. Even though Dad was well qualified and enjoyed the work of a chemist, it did not make a lot of sense to return to the lab when he could make ten times as much money creating and selling test prep booklets with far greater long-term security and less personal risk of explosions.

(8) Maintain a low overhead. Milt started out with the corner of an office. When he expanded, he was able to get a great deal on taking over a lease and purchasing used equipment at a bargain price. He was not concerned about the relatively shabby appearance of this used equipment or the fact that the previous owner had recently died.

(9) Appreciate beauty. Dad really did appreciate the beauty and care of the lettering for Abraham and Rosenfeld Company, Inc. Preserving this beauty also saved him some money, and as part of the myth imbued the sense that in every event in life there is an opportunity to profit from one's ingenuity. No matter how small the profit might be (i.e., the cost of renaming and repainting the door sign), it is worth the effort for the shear creativity of it and small savings will eventually add up.

(10) Never look back. Dad never second-guessed himself through the process of whether or not he was doing the right thing in abandoning his chemistry career that he had worked so hard to create. He was enjoying the process of creating and selling the test prep books, being his own boss, and finding ways to expand on his initial concept.

(11) Expand on a good idea. Dad was never one to sit on his laurels. Someone else might have been content to make a few thousand dollars from the initial motor vehicle operator's booklet and then return to the chemistry lab. Not Dad. When he found a good thing, he wanted more of it. This

led to the armed forces test prep book and in turn that led to expanding the concept to preparing test prep books for all New York City civil service jobs. Once he figured out the printing and distribution side of selling the first two books, he realized that with more titles he could leverage these initial relationships and sell all kinds of related books.

These are simple basic lessons, and Milt utilized them again in growing the business and, as we shall see in chapter four, in rebuilding the business after some unfortunate decisions and circumstances.

CHAPTER 4

BACK FROM THE BRINK
OF BANKRUPTCY

The Role of Magic in Business and the
Ability to Turn Information into Luck

In the late 1930s and into early 1940 and 1941, Arco enjoyed unmitigated growth and prosperity. Dad hired his best friend from City College to serve as editor-in-chief, expanded into larger quarters, still on Park Avenue, and generally lived a carefree and pleasure-filled life. He expanded the test prep side of the business into a full list of civil service occupations including office clerk carrier, fireman, and other mainstream national job occupations. He also took some of his excess cash and began publishing in other areas as well, primarily in the how-to nonfiction areas. His contemporaries were Nat Wartels, the founder of Crown Books a few years earlier; Max Simon of Simon and Schuster; Bennett Cerf of Random House; and many others from those heydays of American book publishing.

Dad was not bred to blueblood stock nor the gentile manners then common in New York publishing circles, but his background proved to be an asset as he was unshackled by the general feeling that publishing was a gentleman's profession in which the unabashed pursuit of market share and dollars was somehow less than dignified. Dad saw dollars everywhere and he pursued them.

If he published a book about dogs, he would venture into pet stores and suggest that they sell them. If Macy's were attracting customers, he would suggest that they sell books as well. This was innovative marketing back in the late 1930s.

But Dad was not a compulsive worker either. He would close the office and take off to see a ball game in the middle of the day, or rearrange his work schedule to accommodate social events. He was a millionaire, unattached, and except for providing a job for his father, pretty much footloose and fancy free as far as his personal economic obligations. Then out of the blue came Pearl Harbor, World War II, and conscription.

My dad's high school friend was a conscientious objector, so without much thought he was left in charge as Dad went off to Fort Benning for basic training. When word came that he would be shipping out, he figured there was a distinct possibility that he might not return, so he made two dramatic decisions. The first was to marry the woman he had been dating for the last several years, who turned out to be my mom. The second was as unwise a decision as was wise the decision to marry Mom. He gave his friend and editor-in-chief a $50,000 bonus on the assumption that he might not return, since he wanted to be sure that his friend was rewarded for his faithful years of service.

Dad had a great time during the war. He was in Stars and Stripes as a communications expert and was also chief mess sergeant for his platoon. He had his near misses, including being one of only a few dozen survivors from a boat of officers torpedoed in the English Channel by the Germans. (He loved to recount that as the boat was going down in the freezing water he kept his head, and instead of jumping ship and dying almost immediately in the frozen water, as some of his fellow soldiers did, he proceeded to fill his knapsack with sacks of rice, beans, and other foodstuff on the theory that if he and others were to survive they would require nourishment. When a small French frigate risked its own survival by coming to their rescue, he was able to jump aboard, and the relatively soft knapsack to cushion his fall.)

As mess sergeant, Dad ended up in France, and when through a typographical error he received rations for 600 men when only sixty were stationed at his camp, instead of trying to alert the army bureaucracy to its error he decided to start bartering the extra cans of Spam, cigarettes, and chocolate bars with the French peasants for fresh chickens, milk, and butter. According not only to him but also to such noted war veterans as author Joseph Heller, Dad served some of the best food in France either before, during, or after the war.

When the war ended and Dad returned to New York, he was in for some rude surprises. His beloved Arco was basically bankrupt. The assets were outweighed by debts with the negative balance a whopping $100,000 dollars, a good sum of money in 1946. Apparently, his editor-in-chief, though a good editor, was an unwise businessperson. He had hired a business administrator who turned out to be a crook. In addition to selling off Arco's ration of paper on the black market for his personal gain (preventing Arco from printing books under contract), he entered contracts with nonperforming book authors in exchange for kickbacks equal to large percentages of the advances he was paying out. Apparently the editor-in-chief had been called upon to perform his substitute military service away from New York, and on short notice, he had not been able to check on this administrator's honesty or track record.

Arco's accountant counseled Dad to declare bankruptcy and close the doors. "I just don't see how you can make this work. Even if you get out of debt you'll be last in line to get paper allotments, since the paper suppliers as well as the printers are going to want cash up front based on your delinquencies, even if you pay them off." Dad was definitely sobered to learn this, and as he had not set aside any money for a rainy day or other calamity, was seriously thinking about following the accountant's advice.

When he went home to discuss his options with his bride, she was not at all responsive to the concept of shutting down Arco to start a liquor store or other easy to run, likely to be profitable business that my Dad suggested. "Milton Gladstone. When I married you, you were a book publisher and a book publisher is what you'll remain. You just find a way to keep the company going. I didn't marry you to be the wife of a liquor store owner." My dad loved my mom, and although he wasn't stuck on remaining a book publisher (after all he only entered the field by accident in the first place), he did want to make her happy and decided to keep his options open to see if some solution might present itself.

My parents were living in Manhattan at the time and that evening was the annual festival in Little Italy (well portrayed in the film *The Godfather Part II*). Along with great food stands, there were other stands selling merchandise and also a soothsayer with a crystal ball. She was only charging a quarter, and Mom suggested that they have her read their fortune. Next thing you know, Dad is sitting in front of a crystal ball and the fortuneteller is saying, "I see a boat and lots and lots of paper and great, good fortune." Milt looked at Selma and Selma looked at Milt with puzzled expressions as they left asking the same unstated question—"What the hell do you make of that?"

A few days went by and the question was soon answered by a phone call from Lester David, an Army friend of Dad's still stationed in Washington with Stars and Stripes. "Milt, a memo just came across my desk that I think will interest you. They collected all the excess unused paper from all the military installations throughout the Pacific from the end of the war and shipped it all to Honolulu, where they are going to hold an auction next week. The memo was supposed to have been published several months ago, but apparently there was a snafu and the memo is only going into the publishing process now. It won't even reach the general public until after the auction date." Well, this was the break Milt had been hoping for. He knew that all the publishers in New York were desperate for paper. The paper mills just couldn't gear up production fast enough to meet the latent demand. With little publicity and few buyers, Milt figured he could buy the paper at a bargain basement price and resell it off the dock in New York. He still had the problem of raising the cash to buy the paper, but he had some business credibility based on the early success of Arco, and found a commodity trader (perhaps Mr. Abraham from whom he first rented office space in 1936) willing to back him for a percentage of the profits.

Within days, Milt hopped a plane for the then long journey to Hawaii and made it just in time to place the winning bid on the entire allotment of paper. He then camped out at the Royal Hawaiian for the next month while he arranged to lease a freighter, hire the stevedores, and load up the ship with the paper, and find additional goods to fill the rest of the ship. By the time he got to the dock in New York he had already sold off all the paper (except the portion he wanted to retain for Arco's own publishing) to other New York publishers for a handsome profit, was able to pay back the commodity broker/lender, and still had $50,000 left to cover half of the Arco debts still outstanding. The other $50,000 was offered up by the editor-in-chief, who saved the bonus from a few years ago before the war started. For the $50,000, the editor-in-chief requested a 50 percent stake in Arco, and since they had been friends since grade school Dad felt that it wouldn't matter anyway, and agreed without really contemplating what would happen if there were ever a falling out between the two friends. The falling out didn't come for several years, but when it did this 50/50 arrangement ended up playing a pivotal role not only in the future of the company but in my own future as well.

With the full repayment of Arco's debts, it did not take long to return the company to profitability. Civil service jobs were increasing rapidly, and the need for civil service test prep books grew even faster. New opportunities presented themselves as well. One of them related to international travel. Soon after the war, the Frankfurt Book Fair was established. Since Dad had enjoyed his European experiences during the war and had made many friends with members of the French Resistance, he was eager to return and the Frankfurt Book Fair was the perfect excuse. Once again Arco had money in its coffers, and in European book publishing, money was the scarcest of all commodities after the war. British publishers would bring by exquisite books that were due to be printed, but the publishers had run out of money. They offered fabulous deals for US distribution rights to the books, if someone would just pay the printer's bill. That someone was often my dad. Soon after that, the idea of standardized tests for college, graduate, and professional schools was accepted, and in addition to publishing civil service test prep, academic test prep books joined the Arco list.

About this time I was conceived, which brings us to the main character in our story. But first let's examine some of the lessons that can be learned from the destruction and resurrection of Arco.

Lessons to Be Learned:

(1) Never give up. The logical course of action was what the accountant suggested: close the doors and declare bankruptcy. Partially at my mom's insistence, Dad resolved to persevere.

(2) Remain open and optimistic. Once Dad resolved to keep his options and the doors open, he kept his mind open to unexpected opportunities—the Lester David phone call.

(3) Be open to magic as long as it doesn't cost too much. The fortuneteller really did tap into some mystical magic. She saw a potential course of action that became a reality. Even though skeptical, my parents were intrigued by the fortuneteller, and no doubt Dad envisioned his course of action in going to Hawaii more readily than he might have without that odd additional bit of motivation.

(4) Be pragmatic. Dad knew he needed cash and that he needed to demonstrate the practical course of action in going to Hawaii. He immediately contacted a trader/broker with both the cash and the expertise on how to formulate a plan to transport the paper if purchased.

(5) Don't be afraid to venture into new realms. Dad had never hired stevedores or leased a ship. It became apparent that this would be necessary to execute the plan. He didn't get flustered, he just did it.

(6) Once the plan is formulated, improve it. Dad increased his profitability by realizing that he would have extra space on the freighter, and needed to seek other goods to transport from Hawaii to New York as well.

(7) Listen to friends. Lester David made the call. Dad listened and trusted Lester's judgment that the auction would be sparsely attended and that a low bid would win the day.

(8) Don't rely too much on friends. A poor choice developed from trusting his best friend and editor-in-chief with running the company in his absence.

(9) Don't panic in the face of disaster. One of the reasons my dad delighted in telling the story of the sinking ship was that it illustrated his constant theme of calm in the middle of a storm. This same quality was essential for dealing with the heavily indebted ship of Arco that he found upon his return.

(10) Assume that you will survive the present disaster, and prepare for your survival. Not only did the foresight of filling the knapsack with food pay off after boarding the small frigate where there were not enough rations for the newcomers as well as the original crew, but the foresight in keeping enough paper for Arco's resurrection after the paper deal was also a lifesaver that helped the company pull out of its near decline.

(11) Marry a strong woman who knows what she wants and knows that what she wants is best for you as well. Of course, if you are a woman, the advice would read marry a man with the same qualities. My mom had high standards as to what she thought was appropriate behavior as well as occupation and environment for her family. There would have been nothing wrong with becoming a liquor storeowner, but it certainly wouldn't have been the highest and best use of my dad's talents and experiences after the war. (By that time, it had been over ten years since Dad had tinkered with chemicals and that career was no longer an option.)

(12) Don't be squeamish about the need to make money. Whether it was opening up new markets for books or taking advantage of the economic misery of exquisite European publishers, Dad was never shy about the fact that the fundamental purpose of his business was to make money. This did not mean that Dad was unconcerned with other aspects of the business or lacked a social conscience (he was philanthropic in unexpected ways and eventually established a chair in chemistry at his alma matter, City College of New York), but he was focused on the idea that making money was a good thing and something that should rightly be the primary obligation of a book publisher. Of course, this seems commonplace now, but in the early forties in New York publishing, this focus on making a profit was somewhat brazen and noteworthy.

CHAPTER 5

IN THE BEGINNING

Earliest Examples from Childhood
of Creating My Own Luck

Soon after the resurrection of Arco it was apparent that the company would survive and prosper and that eventually an heir would be required to run the company. This was not the only reason I was conceived, but it was not a minor factor either. I was born in December of 1949 and had a relatively uneventful childhood. There were some early peculiarities about me from the start. I was an amazingly calm and trusting infant. Anyone at all could come along and hold me and I would never cry. This was the report I received from my mother, as my earliest memories don't go back quite that far. Another unusual characteristic was that I did not seem to grasp the capacity to speak at the normal developmental stage. I was going on five or six and still did not speak in a manner coherent to anyone except my mother. This caused some concern and it was thought that perhaps I was retarded. A couple of years of work with a speech therapist solved the problem, and it turned out that rather than retarded I was on the high end of the intelligence scale after all. I remember one particular gift that was quite unusual. Even in those early years as a toddler I could add, subtract, and multiply and divide double- and triple-digit numbers in my head. It seemed to be an ability with which I was born. I also remember contemplating the concept of infinity and other strange mathematical and philosophical constructs that defied Piaget's prediction of when children are capable of abstract thought and concepts.

Another unusual quality was my ability to run extremely swiftly and to immediately take charge of any group of toddlers with whom I was placed. I was generally athletic and excelled at most sports and games. In addition to my quickness, I seemed to have an extraordinary sense of anticipating where the ball or opponents might be headed. In cards and games of chance I always seemed to draw the card or roll that I needed when I needed it. This was most distressing to my opponents. The cynics often thought that I was cheating, but my friends just started to realize that I had extraordinary good luck at these games of chance. My own explanation was and is that I had extraordinary powers of concentration even as a toddler and that by sheer force of will I would generate the exact roll I needed, be it at Monopoly or Parcheesi or any dice game. The same was true of crazy eights, hearts, and other card games that I played. This ability manifested itself often, and the running joke in the family was that they should send me to Las Vegas to test my talents. It's possible that to some extent I was doing mathematical calculations similar to those evidenced by Dustin Hoffman in the film *Rain Man,* and although that may have been a part of my ability to create my own luck, there was definitely something more than the mere ability to calculate the odds of different occurrences.

I remember one of my finest moments in creating my own luck at the tender age of six at the Phillips Memorial Hospital fundraiser in Sleepy Hollow, New York. My mom was on the committee and had to spend much of the afternoon tending one of the booths. The fair contained many games of chance as well as booths with food and other activities. Tickets were worth either five or ten cents with purchases pegged to either a dime or a quarter. My mom bought me some script and let me wander on my own. I had about two dollars' worth of script at my disposal, and I used up all but a single five-cent ticket.

I was disappointed to discover that there was nothing you could do with just five cents, since the minimum for any attraction was a dime. I wandered around until I came to the "wheel of fortune." I explained to the ticket taker that I only had five cents left, and not a dime, but that I would like to place the ticket on a number. There were sixty numbers on the wheel, and very few winners for the prizes that were awarded for a winning bet. The woman tending the booth looked at me and smiled and said, "Sure, what number would you like?" I bet on number 29 and she gave the wheel a spin. Magically the wheel stopped at number 29, and I won a small bow and arrow set for my nickel chance.

I went back with glee to show my prize to my mother, who was quite delighted that I had been able to occupy myself with rides and attractions for close to two hours on the initial two dollars' worth of script. She needed to tend her booth for at least another hour, so she provided me with another dollar's worth of script and sent me on my merry way. Again, I spent all of my script except for a single five-cent ticket. I returned again to the spinning wheel, and repeated my request that I might be permitted to play with but half the normal amount. Again, I was granted an opportunity to place my bet. This time I chose the number five. And as luck would have it, that number appeared. The actual odds of winning twice in a row out of 60 numbers were one in three thousand six hundred. I did not find this remarkable at the time, as I was used to having good luck and this occurrence only seemed a further manifestation of that to which I deemed myself entitled.

This incident may seem trivial, yet it represents on a deeper level an inner conviction and attitude that has shaped much of my life, particularly my business dealings and attitude toward the material world and the manifestation of material abundance. At a core level, I have always felt that I could generate my own luck and magic. I never felt that long odds alone should dictate whether or not to engage in an activity or enterprise. I expected magic on a daily basis and felt that I had a personal relationship with the keeper of good fortune and that my primary obligation in order to manifest this good luck was to merely concentrate on my desired results. I must say that this ability was strongest as a very young child, when my mind was uncluttered with the cares and programming of adult life. And yet as we shall see in later chapters, I have never entirely lost this belief in my personal access to good fortune or the importance of my own will in helping to manifest good luck.

From the age of seven through twelve, I led a normal childhood. I excelled at sports, particularly Little League, where I starred as the league's best fielding shortstop and base stealer. I never made an error in the three years I played, and was never tagged out stealing base. I wasn't much of a hitter, for, as we later learned, I was nearsighted and should have been wearing corrective lenses. By the time, I made it to junior high I was wearing glasses, and my hitting came around as well. My fielding continued to be flawless, and my range improved along with my quickness. I received the greatest accolades for my fielding and was considered the "vacuum cleaner," so sure handed was I with any ball that came my way. I mention this accomplishment because it too set the tone for much of what I would later accomplish in the business world. I expected to be perfect and to never make an error. The idea of making an error never occurred to me. I learned to anticipate where balls would be hit and would start moving toward them either right before or simultaneous with the actual crack of the hitter's bat. Again, as with concentrating on the cards and dice, I seemed to have a sixth sense that would direct me to where the ball was going to be almost before it was hit. I do not believe that this ability to anticipate in sports was unique to me, and I would venture that all the truly great athletes have been able to cultivate a similar ability. This ability to anticipate is extremely useful in deal making and throughout business. Like the athlete's ability to cultivate anticipation in sport, I believe that anticipation in business can also be cultivated as well.

By the time I was in junior high, I was sent to an all-boys boarding school that focused almost exclusively on sports and studies. I seemed to excel at everything. I went two years without ever making a mistake on a math or science problem; was elected president of my class; was captain of the football, wrestling, and baseball teams; was valedictorian; and won most of the major prizes at commencement. This did not come without some effort, as I applied myself diligently to my studies, but I found the challenges of being the best at whatever I was doing stimulating and enjoyable.

By the time I entered the ninth grade, I was ready for new challenges. One of these challenges was to try to make the varsity wrestling team as a freshman. This required losing a significant amount of weight in order to compete at the lightest weight class, where our championship team required an extra wrestler. In retrospect, it was probably a foolish thing to do, given the health risks, but even at the age of fourteen I was as determined as could be. I met my weight goal and went on to win most of my matches, with the highlight of my career being a tie with the New York state wrestling champion in my weight class. This and other wrong-headed attempts to excel in the extreme alerted me to the need for more radical change. The end result was that I discovered a junior year abroad program for high school students, and sent in an application to spend the 11th grade living with a family in Barcelona, Spain, while attending the Phillips Academy Andover program of School Year Abroad.

My Spanish was somewhat primitive when I arrived, but after several months of isolating myself from my American classmates (except during school hours) and surrounding myself with only native speakers, I soon became fluent. Some of my fondest memories of that year include learning to ski in the Pyrenees and playing on a Spanish baseball team. In both instances, the camaraderie with my teammates and fellow skiers did more for my Spanish ability than any of the classes.

I mention these details of my youth and education because they play an important role not only in my formation but also in highlighting the characteristics that I associate with my later success: my willingness to focus on a goal and go after it no matter what the sacrifices might be, my willingness to try new things and seek new challenges, and my willingness to take a risk on going somewhere totally foreign where I didn't even speak the language.

The most important lesson I learned in Spain was that it was possible to make great progress in achieving fluency in Spanish without working hard and that there was no conflict between having fun pursuing that which I enjoyed most at that time (sports and girls) and achieving the results that the teachers wanted (fluency in Spanish). I also learned to really enjoy life. I had the realization as a student in Barcelona that although English was a wonderfully precise language well suited to business, the Spanish language contained romance and poetry with a kind of magic that could be felt in the Spanish culture and people. In English I was goal-oriented and achievement conscious, whereas in Spanish I was more process oriented, enjoying the moment and living in the present for the experience of life, as well as for my goals. I believe that this is indicative of other European cultures—though disappearing rapidly as American culture and values begin to permeate the coming one-world culture—and is another ingredient of balance in life that has great applicability to business as well.

In a profound way, my ability to balance Spanish and English is indicative of an ability to balance left and right brain activities simultaneously and to hold both with respect and esteem. This talent for integrated thought processing of both the intuitive and analytical halves of the brain is a key component to being the deal and creating your own luck in business. Let me explain the process.

The first stage is to be innocently in the flow—i.e., as a child, just playing a game or participating in an activity that has been placed before you. At a certain point, you begin to take the game seriously and concentrate on your desired result. If you are going to play, you are going to play to win. At the same time, you realize it is just a game, and do not attach too much importance to the outcome. You go back and forth between these two states of analyzing your desire, calculating the odds, desiring your specific result, and just enjoying the process of the play. Somehow, magically, this back and forth technique, which for the most part is unconscious, creates a vortex of energy that manifests the desired good luck. Other examples of this process will be introduced in future chapters directly related to business practices and success, but let us complete the discussion of my early education.

Upon my return from Spain, I enrolled in Phillips Academy Andover for my senior year. It was awkward being a one year senior and having to give up all the freedoms I had enjoyed as an exchange student in Spain. Although there were some great teachers, the experience after Barcelona was anticlimactic. I focused on adapting to the intensely competitive environment at Andover and completing the college admission process. At the time, my first choice was Stanford, with Harvard and Yale included just in case. I was choosing Stanford for the wrong reasons, since I had never been to California nor really examined its programs. At the time, my girlfriend was supposed to move to Palo Alto and that was my overriding motivation. My mother wanted me to go to Yale, and I was thinking that if I didn't go to Stanford, I should probably go to Harvard. As it turned out the only school that wanted me was Yale, so that's where I headed.

Before heading for Yale, I had a summer in front of me and the need to make some extra cash to build up some reserves for college spending and dating money. I was working at Arco in the shipping department and was totally underwhelmed with the experience. The city was hot and the work was monotonous. One Friday, I got a call from a good friend of mine. He was headed to upstate New York for a rock concert of some kind. I didn't know who was playing or what was happening, but it seemed like more fun than spending a hot weekend in New York, so I told him I would go with him. "I'm not sure we can pick up an extra ticket in advance because they say it's sold out, but I'm sure when we get there we'll work out something." Four hours later, we were in bumper-to-bumper traffic on a highway headed for Woodstock. About twelve miles from the venue, we pulled the car off to the side of the road and decided to walk. The experience was everything they show you on that film about Woodstock, and more. The ambience was electric and friendly beyond belief. It really felt like "Woodstock Nation," and the best part was the townspeople along the route, who were so curious and generous toward this ragtag army of love children, hippies, and zoned-out druggies.

It ended up pouring rain, and we didn't stay for the entire concert of three days, but I did meet another friend during the concert who invited me to spend some of the vacation with him up at his parent's house on a little island in the middle of Lake Placid. I thanked him for the invitation, but warned him that it seemed unlikely. I didn't have a car and didn't think I could get up there, but if I did, I would call.

The following weekend, an extremely attractive young woman, who was also spending the summer working at Arco, asked me if I wanted to go with her up to Lake George. I had been talking about my friend in Lake Placid and his invitation, and she suggested that Lake George was relatively close, and, once there, I could probably hop a bus to Lake Placid. I wasn't really all that interested in going to Lake Placid, but I did want to spend some more time with this attractive young lady, so I decided to accompany her on the trip. We had a good ride, but I didn't develop the closer intimacy I was hoping for and learned during the trip that her college boyfriend was meeting her at the lake. The excuse for the trip became the only reason for the trip, and I found a payphone and called my friend, wanting to know if the offer was still good. It was, and I caught the bus and a few hours later was being picked up at the dock, headed toward the summerhouse on the lake.

I had a great time and really got along well with my friend and his parents, and they seemed to sincerely regret having to tell me that the grandparents were headed up for the next two weeks, and would need the guestroom I was occupying. By now I was determined not to return to the hot city, and when they recommended that I go to the Mt. Marcy Hotel to seek employment (since employment would include a place to stay, as well as three meals a day), it seemed like a good idea. Next thing I knew I was hired to work in the kitchen of the famous hotel. My assignment was slop man. This was the bottom of the bottom in terms of the hierarchy of kitchen employment. The job entailed taking the dirty plates full of food straight from the busboy trays, dumping the uneaten food into the garbage, and then rinsing the plates before handing them off to be loaded onto the conveyor belt washing apparatus. The most disgusting part of the job was the frequent need to unclog the drain in the sink where the dishes were initially rinsed. It was impossible to prevent food that stuck to the plates from falling into this drain, and every half an hour or so it would be necessary to clear it out with one's hand. I remember one time in particular, when no matter how hard I tried, I just couldn't get the drain clear. The burly foreman came over, cleared it out, and in his most condescending voice said, "OK, college boy, see if your degree will help you clean this." I felt like telling him that I hadn't even matriculated in college yet, but he really seemed to enjoy his obvious superiority to a college boy in his ability to do what I and my ilk couldn't.

I barely returned for the second day of work, because I really did find the job disgusting, but I had met a charming girl in one of the Lake Placid town shops, who was also a bassoonist. Elsie the bassoonist and I were having too good a time for me to so quickly give up my plan to remain in Lake Placid and avoid the hot city. The second morning, as I was eyeing the clean dish side of the conveyor belt with longing, to my great amazement the foreman came over and in his snarling best said, "College boy, we need another worker on the clean and store side of the conveyor—get over there." Apparently, one of the other workers had quit and the conveyor line was falling behind. What happened next was good fortune beyond belief. The pastry chef (whose apple strudel and other breakfast pastries were the fame of the restaurant) came by and started berating the foreman. "If you don't get me a helper immediately, I will quit. I've had enough of these bums you send me. I need a full time worker, and someone who is clean." Well, the foreman looked around, and there I was. In an exasperated motion, he called me over, pointed to the pastry chef, and said, "Tomorrow, you report to Ingolf, six A.M. sharp. Don't be late."

This was altogether good news. In two days I had moved from slop man to clean and store to pastry washer. I shared my good news with Elsie the bassoonist, and also let on that now, although I had to start at six A.M., I could also be off work by two. Well, the next morning Ingolf and I hit it off just fine. He was grateful to have me, and I was grateful to be free of the conveyor belt line and the threat of returning to the slop side of the line. I started cleaning bowls and utensils, but soon graduated to entering the freezer to retrieve dough, to pouring apple mix from cans into the famous strudel (I was appalled), and to squeezing out the cream for the pastry cream puffs. After two days of this, Ingolf came to me and said, "I like your work. From now on, you are going to be my assistant." Well, I liked the new title, but there was no increase in pay, and all this meant was that now, in addition to everything else, I had to crack the eggs and do a lot of other extra work that was really starting to seem excessive. Two days later, I received my paycheck and was also told by Ingolf that the next day was his day off, and I would be in charge all by myself. I thought this absurd and told him so, but he insisted. I told him that this made no sense and that I would quit if he insisted. He insisted. I quit. I went to tell Elsie that I was going to have to leave, but first I stopped by my friend's house where I had been staying. His parents greeted me warmly and told me that the grandparents were going to have to leave later that afternoon, and if I wanted to, I could return as their guest. Well, that was just great, and I spent the rest of the summer up there escaping the heat of the city, with plenty of spending money from that week of time and overtime during my meteoric career rise from slop man to assistant pastry chef at the Mt. Marcy Hotel.

But as the song says, "All good things must end someday." I made my good-byes to Elsie the bassoonist and headed for Yale. I wasn't too thrilled about actually going to Yale, and I ended up withdrawing after the first semester. With the protests and turmoil relating to the Vietnam War and the general drug culture around me, I felt lost as to my sense of purpose. I was spending most of my first semester at Yale just going to the movies, since I discovered that there was a different film society every night on campus showing at least one film, if not double or triple features. I must have averaged at least ten films a week during those first few months. I particularly remember the odd films chosen by the Yale Law School Film society, as well as the Ingmar Bergman film festival put on by my residential college, Berkeley.

In any event, other than the movies that first semester seemed like a waste, and if I were going to drift, I might as well drift without paying tuition. I drifted until the following year, with a sojourn in the south of France, and then decided to return. I was still drifting, but I decided I preferred to drift at Yale, rather than in Vietnam. With Black Panther riots, anti-ROTC demonstrations, and other distractions, I did not have the stereotypical "by the tables down at Maury's" carefree Yale existence of song and lore. In fact, the place was downright tense. I never really focused on a major, and spent the next two years taking nothing but introductory courses, except advanced classes in Spanish literature, which I loved and which were particularly easy for me given both my fluency in Spanish and background in literature. I had been intending to major in math, since that had always been my strongest academic subject, but I drew first an Indian and then an Australian math professor—the first whose language was impossible for me to understand and the second whose mathematical notation was quite different from that which I had studied previously. In both cases, it was for a required third level of calculus that had to be completed before qualifying for the fun stuff, like Robinson's Number theory, and in the end, with the riots and all, math just didn't seem too significant in the big picture. I was into a relatively lazy phase and just decided that I didn't want to be bothered with learning some new notation to manipulate formulas in n dimensions that I could already manipulate in three dimensions. Right or wrong, I walked away from my future as the world's next great mathematician, the academic destiny that my early math teachers had already prognosticated.

So there I am, ready to enter my junior year at Yale, off on a summer sojourn to Salamanca, Spain, when I learn that my father has had a massive heart attack and that, although he has pulled through, it is unlikely that he will live more than another five years at most.

Upon my return, my dad and I have a heart to heart (which was unusual, since up to that point my dad and I had never had a heart to heart), and I learn that "Your mother wouldn't agree, but I think that you have had enough schooling and that it is time for you to finish up and get into the business." This was somewhat of a shock, as it was already September and classes were starting in less than a week. I inquired further and learned that it would be OK to complete one more year of school, but that the goal was that I should graduate in one year rather than two and make arrangements so that this could happen. Ever the dutiful son, I did. I activated some advanced placement credits, pushed the limit of my course load from four to six courses a semester, and elected Spanish literature as my default major, since that was the only field in which I had taken more than a single class my first two years at Yale. That proved to be a pretty hectic year, but I later learned that the reason that my dad was so eager for me to graduate and join him at Arco was because he had negotiated a buy/sell agreement with his partner, former friend, and editor-in-chief, which dictated a relatively low price at which Arco would be sold should one of the principals die. Since my father's health was now fragile, it seemed imperative to have someone from the family helping to run the business in case anything should happen to "dear old Dad." Some clause in their agreement would defer the sale of the company as long as a direct relative was representing one side or the other as an active member of the company.

Despite the increased course load, I managed to graduate *cum laude,* with highest honors in my major, and the William DeForrest Prize for the best essay in the Spanish language. By the time I reported for work that summer, Dad was much healthier, and he decided that I would be most useful understudying his editor-in-chief, with whom relations had so deteriorated that he now worked out of a special editorial office fifty miles away from the company's center in Manhattan. The theory was that I should see how the editorial system worked, so that Dad could buy out the editor without losing any expertise on how to put the test prep books together most efficiently.

The editorial offices were in the former honeymoon cottage on the Vanderbilt estate at the train station in Scarborough, New York. The editorial offices were called The Production Company, which was really a joke, given the low level of production of anything useful that came out of that office. In fairness, there was no question that the editor in charge was truly a genius. He spoke seven or nine languages and seemed to know a little bit about everything. He had also created a unique system of producing and revising test prep books as if they were moving parts in an automobile manufacturing plant. In theory, the system was brilliant, and it was ingenious. The trouble was that he had fallen in love with the system, and lost sight of the necessity of updating material, rather than just cleverly filing, storing, and retrieving it. To some extent, he had created a giant computer memory system, in which there were files on each and every kind of question that could be retrieved at will and put together to form any of a hundred different civil service and college-level test prep books. The trouble was that he was so into saving each and every section so that it could be used in multiple books, he was not actually updating any of the material, some of which dated back to the 1930s when the company had first started. This was 1972, so even math problems were often ridiculous, quoting prices of a loaf of bread for a nickel or a car for $750.

It took me about two weeks to realize that the entire production company was doing nothing but recycling obsolete material. I told this to my dad, and recommended that he immediately buy out his partner, since nothing would be lost, and much money could be saved by eliminating his unnecessary though admittedly ingenious operation. Dad was not in a position to immediately effect a buyout, so I struggled on for several months editing material that didn't need editing but to just be discarded and continually annoying my immediate employer, my dad's partner. This soon proved intolerable to both of us, and it was decided that I would work out of my house revising one of the key titles: *How to Score High on the Medical College Admission Test*. While I was doing this, Dad would get it together so that a buyout could occur, and I would be given the opportunity to create a more efficient editorial process for revising the hundreds of titles in test prep that were the key assets of Arco.

Lessons to Be Learned:
My earliest years:
(1) Focus and concentration can help create luck.
(2) Hard work pays off.
(3) It is good to take chances and seek new challenges.
(4) Taking the path of least resistance often leads to positive results.
(5) Always do what you enjoy and you will make progress.
(6) Focus on getting the job you want and it might just happen.
(7) Be open to unexpected coincidences.
(8) Don't be afraid to get your hands dirty.
(9) Don't be afraid to quit if you are not doing something you love.
(10) Don't be afraid to abandon an area of great expertise (in my case math) if exercising that expertise no longer has meaning.
(11) Honor your parents.
(12) Don't be controlled by your parents' wishes.

Key Insight:
BE AWARE OF YOUR APTITUDES

CHAPTER 6

THE AMAZING INCREDIBLE JOURNEY

In Search of Ancient Mysteries

It was during this period that my life took an unusual twist, which taught me that the good luck I could create as a child could be applied to business as well. In order to keep fit, I had decided that while I was writing the MCAT book I would go to the Westport, Connecticut, YMCA and play paddleball in the men's lunchtime paddleball league. One of the competitors I met there was a man named Fred Warshofsky. Fred was about twenty years older than I was, but a more experienced paddleball player, and we had close games and great competition. We never discussed our work but I knew that he was a writer and a television producer, and he knew that I was a writer and researcher from my brief description of the MCAT project I was completing.

One day, after playing a heated match, he asked me if I had ever heard of Erich von Daniken and his book *Chariots of the Gods*. The truth was that I had not, so he gave me a quick synopsis. He started talking about the Nazca lines and some other phenomenon in Peru, where I had lived one summer in Arequipa working for *Proyecto Amistad,* a person-to-person kind of Peace Corps without any government involvement. I knew and loved the areas he was talking about and shared my enthusiasm of the locations he was planning on visiting for his film project. I didn't think much about it, but the following week when we met to play paddleball, he asked me if I would be interested in helping him with the research on his forthcoming project to be entitled *In Search of Ancient Mysteries*. I said that I would consider it, so he suggested that I meet him the following day in New York City at 747 Third Avenue in the offices of Tomorrow Entertainment, a subsidiary of General Electric Corporation that had just purchased the Alan Landsberg Film Production company, which was slated to make this documentary sequel to von Daniken's *Chariots of the Gods*.

I showed up the next day, and for a twenty-year-old, it was awesome. Fred's office, which he was only using once or twice a week for this project, was bigger than the house I was renting at the time in Westport. It had a huge corner vista of what seemed like all of Manhattan, with numerous support offices of secretaries and others leading up to it. I was used to the shabbier offices of book publishing companies and was impressed. As I sat down on the couch in his office, he handed me a slim binder with a black plastic cover and told me, "There's a lot of smoke in this, but let me know what you think." I looked around at my surroundings and thought, "This is a good gig if you can get it," and despite reading a sixteen-page treatment that seemed farfetched at best, I offered that I could probably get into it. Well, that was basically the end of the meeting, except for some general chit-chat about the structure of Tomorrow Entertainment, and how we would be working in the section of the company that was reserved for the creative, as opposed to the business side of the endeavor. Their offices were actually superior to these, but these weren't too bad, and in any event, I would only be coming into the city once or twice a week, as it was intended that I become the researcher to help flesh out the mostly smoke sixteen-page treatment. These and other observations were provided by Fred, who immediately became my mentor.

The next day I arranged to meet Fred at his home office in Westport. The first thing Fred said to me was, "I'm going to do you a favor that I wish someone had done for me when I was your age. I am going to call Alan Landsberg and have him hire you as my research assistant for this project. The budget only calls for a hundred dollars a week, but I'm going to get you $125. Is that alright?" Well, that was somewhat less than I was making working as writer/editor for Arco, but I realized that I could do both jobs simultaneously, so without really caring about how much I would be paid at all, I just shrugged and said, "Sure, thanks." Fred called Alan Landsberg on the speakerphone and told me to listen, but not to speak. This was 1972, and I had never seen a speakerphone. Landsberg seemed rather brusque. His only question was, "Now, he's not a student is he? We don't want any students. He's actually done research, right?" Fred defended me: "Yes. In fact, he's just finishing up the research on a book project right now." "Well, as long as he's not a student. We don't want any students. What's it going to cost us?" "I can get him for $125 a week," Fred replied. "That's high," intoned Landsberg. "Why not a hundred?" "Well, he's a Yale graduate, and he's really good." "Well, just so long as he's not a student, go ahead."

After Fred hung up the phone, he shook my hand and just said, "Congratulations." Little did I know that my brilliant film career was just beginning, and little did Alan Landsberg know that the fact that I was almost still a student proved to be the most valuable asset I would bring to the successful filming of *In Search of Ancient Mysteries.* But that's getting way ahead of what is the fascinating story of what happened next.

As the researcher for *In Search of Ancient Mysteries,* it was my job to help create the shot list for what would be filmed. It was pretty wide open, with a copy of Erich von Daniken's *Chariots of the Gods* handed to me as a point of departure and not much more. I decided to work out of the Westport Public Library, which was next to the YMCA, so that I could continue to play paddleball. In going through the library's resources, I discovered that the library contained every copy of *National Geographic* ever published. I also knew (from an introductory anthropology/archeology course) of some academic books relating to civilizations in Peru, Bolivia, and throughout Latin America. The *National Geographics* were a great resource, and I thought it grand that someone was paying me to go through every issue to look for anything that might be interesting.

As the project had been presented to me, I would have about four months to gather information, determine likely shooting locations, and write letters requesting government permission and related information regarding flying to and filming these ancient mysteries. It was not part of my original contract to have me join the film crew while on location, but of course, that was my secret goal, and I slanted the locations to include a heavy dose of South American sites, where my knowledge of Spanish would be particularly useful for the actual shoot.

Once a week I would meet with Fred to go over the shot list. We were getting close to having a final list, and Fred now wanted me to start going into the city in order to use the Tomorrow Entertainment staff to send out letters requesting permission to film around the world. It was only May, and he did not think that it would be necessary to start shooting until August, so it seemed as though we would have plenty of time.

I went into the office that Monday and started sending out requests for film permissions. I was making good progress when Fred called me into his office,

"Bill, how would you like to go along as advance coordinator to help make the arrangements on location? With your Spanish fluency, I think you could be helpful, particularly in South America." Well, this was what I had been hoping for, so I didn't hesitate to say yes. I was wrapping up my work on the Medical College Admission Test book and had already told my dad that until he could arrange a buyout of his partner, I would be making other employment plans. In addition, I had just recently been accepted to teach at Phillips Academy Andover and was mulling over whether or not to accept that opportunity, which would start the following September. I was concerned about whether or not the shooting schedule would allow me to still accept the Andover position, when Fred dropped a bombshell.

"One small change in the schedule, though. Because of other commitments, we have to start shooting within the next two weeks.

54

We need you to get down to Peru, where the first locations will be, by the end of the week." Since I knew I could wrap up the MCAT book in just a few days, this delighted me. With a twelve-week shooting schedule, it meant that I could still say yes to the teaching position at Andover as well.

It was only later that I realized that few or none of the permission letters had been sent and that leaving without completing all the advance work would probably make my job more difficult. Little did I know.

The excitement of the moment was contagious. A new contract had to be dictated to me over the phone, which I took down word by word on my parents' kitchen table in their house in Greenwich, Connecticut. The contract ended up reading that I was being hired "to search for ancient mysteries anywhere in the world where that search might take me," and they upped my salary to $150 a week. I later learned that my per diem meal money allowance was going to be $35 a day, or 50 percent more than my salary, but the money aspect was really insignificant. I was being given an opportunity to go around the world with all expenses paid to some of the most exotic locations imaginable. I wasn't even sure where I would be going because the final shot list had still not been approved by Landsberg productions back in Hollywood, and the total range of locations included Israel, England, Greece, Australia, India, Japan, Hawaii, and locations in France, Italy, and throughout the US. I ended up going to the airport the evening before the flight to Peru to pick up the ticket, and it was a good thing I did because the actual ticket took two hours to write out. It was also a good thing that I had been wired an extra $500 in what they termed "magazine money," since there was a small surcharge on the international ticket due to the fluctuation of the value of the dollar at that time. The surcharge expense alone was over $200.

It did not take me long after landing in Peru to realize that this was going to be a daunting task indeed. The letter requesting permission to film that I had sent the Monday before departing was delivered to the Minister of Culture, with whom I had my first meeting just as I started to meet with him. When I told him we hoped to have the crew and equipment cleared within five days, he simply laughed and said that it was impossible. He was rather amused that I seemed to have no background in film, and he couldn't believe that a major Hollywood movie company would send an amateur such as myself to make such absurd requests.

The film minister was correct up to a point, but in reality it may have been my very ignorance of what was involved and my lack of experience that ignited the circumstances that would lead to the success of the project. I should also add that I had significant help from the executives back at Landsberg, who really did know what they were doing, and who repeatedly came up with ingenious schemes to circumvent impossible government restrictions. In the case of Peru, the solution that was hit upon was to make our project a coproduction with Peru's most successful filmmaker, Bernardo Batievsky. Bernardo had studied at UCLA's film department and was friends with Alan Landsberg. He was the owner of Lima's largest bus company, and in that role had been made an honorary member of the police department, with an actual police badge and identity card. He had also been the person who had drafted the Peruvian film laws that prevented foreign film equipment from being imported into Peru for foreign-financed productions. He had created elaborate bureaucratic hindrances because his goal was to prevent outsiders from making films in Peru without using Peruvian film personnel. By making the production a coproduction with his Peruvian firm, the restrictions didn't apply as far as the film commission was concerned. We were still left with the problem of customs, since the film itself as well as the equipment would have to go through a lengthy process of sitting in customs and being inspected for days, if not weeks. The police badge came to our rescue in circumventing that obstacle, and we were on our way.

But that was just the beginning. I soon discovered that several of the items on my shot list, taken from sources such as Erich von Daniken, didn't really exist, or were dependent upon climactic conditions, such as certain cloud formations at certain times of the year, that were either months behind or ahead of our present shooting schedule. But I didn't let such developments bother me, because in the first place I was only being paid $150 a week, and I already had in hand an around-the-world plane ticket, so the worst that could happen was that I would fail at an impossible task.

In retrospect, I can see that it was this liberating realization and subsequent detachment from the projected goals of the project that enabled me to start thinking "outside of the box." Instead of trying to adapt the reality of Peru to our shot list and preconceived notion of what was required to make a film, I opened up to the actual flow of events around me and more or less just went with that flow moment to moment, without ever letting go of the final goal.

The goal was to get my crew in and out of the country and to arrange to film material that would somehow be related to a story about unexplainable mysteries that might support the von Daniken theory that astronauts from outer space came and did some pretty strange things eons ago, leaving relatively few traces of their stay. I personally never came to fully believe the theory as von Daniken described it in his famous books, but I certainly did come to realize that a great ancient technology from some source had disappeared from the face of the earth and that furthermore, major discontinuities have occurred in the history of the world's great achievements and civilizations.

Meanwhile, I found myself under intense pressure from the director and production manager to not only get as much of what we originally intended to film on film but also to do this efficiently and quickly. We had limited financial resources, limited physical resources, and limited time resources. Specifically, we had to film on five continents in eight countries in less than twelve weeks for what in retrospect was the laughable budget of $200,000. We accomplished this goal, and our success was partly because I was so inexperienced that I didn't understand how impossible the challenge really was. The executives at Landsberg Productions played a major role, as did every member of the film crew, but on a deeper level, the whole production was a success because of everyday miracles and our willingness to let go of any preconceptions about what the final film would be or how the film would be made.

For example, I would show up at pre-chosen locations only to find that people and artifacts described in books were nonexistent. But instead of throwing my hands up in despair, I would breathe into the dilemma, free my mind of preconceptions, start asking questions, and more often than not, find people who had more interesting information than what I had originally been sent to look for. The same nonlinear phenomenon kept happening with objects to be filmed.

After a few days of this strange flow of good luck, I remember consciously turning the whole process over to God—just letting go of my own ego and living in the present moment for the entire production over the next twelve weeks. No matter what happened, no matter how frustrating or impossible a request seemed, I just turned it over to a higher power and said to myself, "If it is meant to be, it will be—we'll find a way."

And seeming miracles kept happening. In India, for instance, it was quite clear that there was no way that the Indian government was going to let us film in the museum in Delhi without paying a major bribe or two—and even then probably stiffing us. The folks back in Hollywood had budgeted seven thousand dollars specifically for "gifts." But I never spent a dime of that money on bribes.

One morning, I walked into the Ministry of Culture in India, only to be told that the only way we could film in the museum in Delhi was if we received permission from the director of the museum first, directing the Minister of Culture to provide the permission letter (which of course he would only do upon receiving a significant bribe).

The director of the museum, however, by one of those curious nonlinear quirks of chance, proved to be an Oxford-educated scholar who had studied at the same University as some of my Yale University professors, and we ended up having some enjoyable scholarly debates as I identified the objects we hoped to film. Everything seemed to be flowing perfectly, but despite the general cheerfulness of our communication, I was not given permission to film. Instead, I was directed to go see B. N. Sharma, the "keeper of the fifteenth century," who was the curator for the objects under discussion.

Staying optimistic, I went to see B. N. Sharma. Rather than being focused on getting the letter of permission from him, I remained neutral to that goal and focused upon personal encounter and friendship. This succeeded perfectly. Over tea, I soon discovered that he had studied at Boston University in an exchange program and that we had some acquaintances in common. One thing led to another, and it being closing time, I was invited to dinner with Mr. Sharma at his home, a forty-minute train ride outside of Delhi. During the course of dinner, we developed genuine heartfelt rapport, and I experienced some incredible conversations with the rest of his Brahmin family on the nature of reality, the role of meditation, and other topics having nothing whatsoever to do with the film project or getting permissions.

Lo and behold, the next day B. N. Sharma submitted a letter of authorization to the museum director but also got the museum director excited about the film itself. Not only did the museum director give the permission letter, he even agreed to go on camera to talk about the ancient Vedic manuscripts in which there are descriptions and blueprints of actual flying machines believed to have been in use in India more than two thousand years ago.

When I returned the next day to the Minister of Culture with the formal letter of authorization, to save face with the director he was forced to give the crew permission to film without receiving a penny. The flow had been immaculate, and I had done zero pushing or manipulation to get exactly what I needed, and much more besides. Therein lies the subtle and essential glory of nonlinear approaches to business.

From this early experience, I garnered certain essential clues regarding how to succeed in business, which I subsequently would apply to starting my own business. First of all, because I had never really been in "the film box" of preordained expectations and procedures, I worked outside of the box almost from the beginning. At a core level, I had no attachment to the success of the project, so I was quite relaxed in the face of repeated failures and apparent dead ends. I never paused or dwelt on the disappointments, but just kept going forward. Most important, step by step I developed the inner certainty that this project had some special purpose far beyond that known by me, the director, the executives at Landsberg Productions, or anyone else—that the ultimate purpose of the project was something far beyond merely making a film and making some money for Mr. Landsberg. I didn't know and to this day can't say that I truly understand the higher purpose of the film, but I think it probably had something to do with exposing tens of millions of people to images of the extraordinary accomplishments of now nonexistent civilizations in a popular way that would get people to really see and think about their own potential and the destiny of our planet.

I know that the film came together magically the way it did only because there was something larger than all of those involved that not only allowed it to happen, but required it to happen. This was my first and most dramatic introduction to this way of thinking about work. Since then, many similar experiences have been repeated throughout my business career and continue to manifest regularly. Some might call such events serendipity, synchronicity, good luck, dumb luck, or just coincidences, but they happen with far too much regularity to be dismissed as pure chance.

I felt then, and continue to feel to this day, an underlying power which moves us when we allow it to move us—an intuitively driven inspiration which is the source of all good luck, insight, and business breakthroughs.

Lessons Learned from Working on *In Search of Ancient Mysteries*

(1) Lack of qualifications and expertise can be a positive rather than a negative.

(2) It is possible to influence events by sheer effort and will.

(3) Influencing events works best if one is not too attached to the outcome.

(4) Honesty at all times is better than bribes.

(5) You can't always get what you want, but if you really try you can probably get what you need.

(6) Being in the moment with people and connecting with them on their level is better than trying to force people to cooperate with you.

(7) It's OK to be helpless and not try to hide your utter ineptitude, if that is really what is going on.

(8) Be open to miracles and you just might experience them. As they say in golf, very few holes-in-one have been made by golfers who aren't aiming at the hole.

(9) It is a good thing to align yourself with individuals and organizations that know what they are doing and have successful track records.

(10) Be flexible in all things.

(11) Be steadfast in your basic values and beliefs. Know what you stand for and rely on that in every instance, and you can trust to be shown what to do next when you haven't a clue on your own.

(12) Always seek the highest and best result for yourself and all with whom you interact, and try to keep your ego out of it.

Key Insight:
DEVELOP A POSITIVE, CAN-DO ATTITUDE

CHAPTER 7

MY BRILLIANT CAREER PHASE ONE: OUT OF WORK AND LOOKING FOR SOMETHING TO DO

Being in the Right Place at the Right Time

After the initial success of the filming of *In Search of Ancient Mysteries,* I was offered an associate producer position on the television spin-off series that the special engendered. I turned it down. I turned it down partly because film was not seen as entirely appropriate work compared to book publishing in my family, and partly because I had always had a desire to teach and had been offered a teaching position at Phillips Academy Andover. The fact that the film job was glamorous and made exactly ten times as much as the teaching position never factored into my decision.

I was proud of what I had accomplished with *In Search of Ancient Mysteries,* and how I had evolved in my own knowledge of the process of creating a film. The director/producer of the shoot, Fred Warshofsky, had been forced to abandon the project in Israel, so I made all the key decisions in both India and Japan. In India, we spent a few extra days, but with the help of the director of the museum in Delhi, we also ended up getting twice as much footage as originally anticipated. This was a good thing, because when we arrived in Japan I was shocked at the huge expense of everything compared to the rest of the world. Also, by now it was August, and travel throughout Japan was very difficult due to the huge amount of summer vacation travel by native Japanese. I made a quick executive decision to abandon 90 percent of the Japanese locations as too inaccessible or too expensive, and sent the crew home early and under budget, much to the delight of the Alan Landsberg accounting department. When it turned out that we had more than enough footage for the television documentary and could in fact produce what they called a four wall version as well (TV transported to theaters and home video), I was a true hero, as this indicated additional heretofore unanticipated revenue streams. The documentary was aired twice a year (every year for close to ten years) and received huge ratings from the get-go.

But despite all this, I chose the teaching position and was glad I did because I learned that I was really only a good teacher for the most advanced and not the average students. I didn't have enough patience to be a great classroom, but at least I learned this. Not sure what to do next, I applied to four or five graduate schools with the thought that I might like to pursue the field of cultural anthropology. Since I had had to condense my last two years at Yale into a single year, I felt somewhat deprived of pursuing what I thought would have been my major in the normal course of events, had my father not asked me to graduate early. Most of the graduate schools looked at my undergraduate record and felt it rather preposterous that I should apply to their programs, given that I only had two semesters of introductory anthropology courses to my credit. But there was one graduate program that did not think that my background in Latin American literature and my casual mention of my esteem for the work of Claude Levi-Strauss was unrelated to their program, and, lo and behold, I was accepted by Harvard University. Not only was I accepted, I was targeted by the chairman of the department, David Maybury Lewis, as his particular student and awarded the highest scholarship package available, which included a National Institute of Mental Health Grant that covered not only all tuition and living expenses but also significant research expenses for travel as well. Again, the luck factor had reared its head. I later learned that I was actually number one on the wait list because of my unorthodox background as a graduate student applicant. When Harvard's top candidate chose the more prestigious anthropology program of Chicago over them, the other four candidates (only five of several hundred applicants were admitted annually) had already locked in their aid packages, and the only package left was this extraordinary fellowship.

It took me about six months at Harvard to learn that I was not suited to be a professor of anthropology. I loved the subject matter and was a stellar student, absolutely flawless, but my dreams of studying primitive peoples and making fascinating discoveries of lost peoples were dashed as I realized that by the late 1970s, there were few if any such peoples left to discover. Anthropology as a profession had degenerated into a glorified study of cross-cultural sociology that was curious about the assimilation of ancient cultures and not their preservation or ethnographies.

The highlight of my Harvard career was teaching non-verbal communication, which turned out to be the most popular social science course in the entire University. Of course, many of the students thought that any course with such a title had to be a "gut" (i.e., easy) course and although they were right, the subject matter was fascinating. I eventually got into a lot of trouble with my colleagues by writing a popular book entitled *How to Test Your Own Mental Health*. This book came about almost by accident and did not meet the academic purity of the department. The book did help a lot of people and further convinced me that academia and I did not fit altogether perfectly.

The idea of the book came to me during a lecture given by a professor of psychology to the tutors of Adam House. There was great concern at Harvard over the relatively large number of suicides among the undergraduates who were under our care and supervision. It was thought that it would be useful to have a psychologist present us with an outline of symptoms and danger signals that we should be alert to as signs of mental and emotional instability among our charges. As I was going through the list of symptoms, I realized that I was mentally ticking off the large number of symptoms that applied to my own mental state at that time. I could see that other graduate students and professors were doing the same. I made an intuitive leap that these very symptoms could be self-applied, and *voila*—test your own mental health. I wrote the book in about six weeks during holidays and thought it a more profitable use of my time than taking on additional tutoring, which I was doing as well. My peers did not see it quite the same, and I could tell that from their point of view I had run amuck.

I now found it hard to keep or replace my advisor and was basically persona non grata. I went ahead and wrote my thesis, but was already mentally gone and never did get around to inserting the footnotes or staying for its defense, as required for the Ph.D. By then I was cured of academia and Arco beckoned again. This time my father assured me that he would make a serious effort to buy out his partner, and told me to start assembling my own editorial team in New York City to replace the Scarborough-based Production Company.

Given my "complete with the experience" relationship with academia, this seemed a suitable time to start taking publishing seriously. I was actually enjoying myself and the challenges of creating an editorial department when I received a call from Hollywood.

"Hello, I'm looking for Bill Gladstone."

"This is Bill Gladstone."

"Is this the Bill Gladstone who went around the world with the Landsberg Productions of *In Search of Ancient Mysteries?*"

"Yes, it is."

"Well, I'm sitting here with Paul, the photographer from that shoot, and he said if we were going to make an international production that included a dozen countries in twelve weeks, we should get Gladstone. Are you interested?"

"That depends. I'm pretty busy right now. What's the picture about?"

"We're calling it *In Search of Jesus Christ*. The film will follow the apocryphal legends about the historical Jesus, including his supposed visits to England, India, and Japan."

"I don't know. I would have to check with my employer. I'm editorial director here, and it won't be easy to get away."

"You can write your own ticket. We really need you."

"Well, I make a lot more money now than I did back then."

"It's really no problem. We can pay you ten times what you were making then. We're ready to go in about two weeks. How about it?"

"Let me think it over, and I'll get back to you tomorrow."

I talked it over with my dad and he still wasn't ready for the complete buyout of his partner, and the editorial team was functioning well enough for the present, so he more or less gave me his blessing to take a leave of absence. Next thing I knew, I was headed around the world all expenses paid to talk to religious leaders, Hindus, and mystics throughout the Mid-East and Asia, including an audience with the Dali Lama of Tibet. I enjoyed the project, more or less, but less than working on the *In Search of Ancient Mysteries* project, because the executive producer of this film was really inexperienced and never got into the flow. I was relieved when we finally left the subcontinent of India, and despite some amazing experiences, including being literally treated as a god and the fulfillment of an ancient Ahmadiyya prophecy, was glad when we arrived at the final stop in Japan.

While in remote parts of India, it had been difficult to communicate with the office back in New York City, and when I finally got through to my secretary long distance from Japan, she asked me, "So what do you think of the sale?" "What sale?" I asked with alarm. "Don't tell me your dad didn't tell you?" she asked incredulously while adding, "He sold the company to Prentice Hall last week." "You're kidding me." "No, I'm serious." "You're kidding." "No. He really sold the company." I hung up in shock and disbelief.

I was destined to run Arco. I gave up my senior year at Yale to be ready if necessary, and the company gets sold without so much as a by your leave. I couldn't comprehend what had happened.

By the time I returned to Manhattan, I was extremely upset. My father, who in his entire publishing career had never allowed anyone except one author when celebrating a bestseller to pay for a business meal (there's a whole etiquette in which publishers always buy lunch for agents, authors, and suppliers, agents buy lunch for authors, etc., that was strictly adhered to in the old days), invited me to lunch to explain what he had done and why. I wasn't in a particularly good listening mood, and I made a point of not only tearing up the contract he had negotiated with the new employer, but also insisted upon paying for the meal as an act of defiance. It did not matter to me that the income was guaranteed for three years with no accountability. This was not what I had been led to believe would be my destiny, and I wanted no part of it. I left in a huff, determined to find my own way without any assistance from my dad who I felt betrayed me.

Several years later, I learned that my dad had had a second heart attack the day that I left the country to work on *In Search of Jesus Christ*. He had not wanted to share that information with me, and, according to him, that really hadn't been the overriding reason for making the sale. He was offered a fair price and he felt that it was the wisest course of action, given the intractability of his partner in his attempts to buy him out. His partner had refused his last offer and said, "Get an outside party to pay that price and I'll take it, but I'll never sell to you." With greater objectivity, I eventually understood and forgave my dad and we became closer than ever, but the immediate aftermath of the selling of Arco was that he and I barely spoke for almost two years.

The first six months after leaving Arco were disorientating. I kept irregular hours, decided to write a novel, and made a small secondary income from late night poker games in a bar in SoHo on Saturday nights from midnight to five A.M. I hung with a strange crowd of UN translators and sympathetic women, and generally was at loose ends. I took a job in Hollywood as executive producer of a movie, but quit after three days when it became apparent that the film leader had no idea what he was doing other than spending his family's fortune. Part of his definition of executive producing included procuring drugs and other illegal substances for himself, his writer, and director, all of whom were chosen to be the best of the best.

Much chagrined, I returned to New York without a real idea of what I should be doing with my life. I was not happy and I seemed to lack direction. I was saved by the needs of others. The first call was from the director of the School Year Abroad program that I had attended in high school. The program was now almost ten years old, and they had decided that it was time to organize an alumni association. Might I be willing to meet with him the following week in Manhattan to discuss his ideas? Well, discuss we did, and next thing I know, I volunteered to organize a dinner for ten or so other New York City–based alumni. Somehow, at that dinner it was decided that we would start the alumni association with those present and that I would be its founding president (since I had organized the dinner). I am proud to say that I served as the president of the SYA Alumni Association for more than twenty-five years and helped raise millions of dollars to give scholarships for international study to hundreds of deserving students from throughout the country.

The process of being needed and helping School Year Abroad got me headed back toward productivity. The next call was from Jerry Rockefeller (no relation to Nelson), who had been responsible for the acquisition of Arco by Prentice Hall, representing the Prentice Hall side of the negotiations. Prentice Hall was at a loss in understanding what to do with Arco now that they had acquired it. Might I not be interested in preparing an action report for new management? Well, I was motivated to do this, for I was still angry with my dad and through this report could pinpoint his numerous weaknesses and the clear idiocy of maintaining the Production Company now that there was a new owner. It was even better when Jerry informed me that the consulting job would pay $5,000, which at that time was much needed by the part time, poker playing, unemployed, semi-derelict that I had become.

It took me all of two days to write that report, but when I called Mr. Rockefeller to turn it in, instead of being pleased, he was aghast. Although he read the report and liked it, he asked, "Isn't there some additional research you can do? I can't justify a fee of $5,000 for you for two days' worth of work." "But I've been living with this company my entire life. I know Arco backwards and forward. This is an accurate plan," I countered.

"I know that, but it says in here that one area of expansion for Arco could be California-based state exams. Why don't you go out there for a week and do a little research," Mr. Rockefeller suggested.

I had friends in California, so I decided that there was some additional research I could do and that going to California for ten days was not such a bad idea. Mr. Rockefeller arranged for the travel expenses to be added to the budget. The night before I was to leave, Miguel Sanchez, the older brother of the Spanish family that I lived with in Barcelona, was in town and invited me to join him for dinner with another close friend of his. The close friend was dating a woman who worked for Harcourt Brace Jovanovich's new division in San Diego, California. He put me on the phone with her and I told her I was headed to LA, and she suggested that I stop by and visit her in Del Mar if I had any extra time.

As it turned out, I did have extra time, and so I drove down to San Diego, visited Harcourt's headquarters, and spent a weekend in Del Mar. Del Mar was and is a truly charming town and I couldn't help but make inquiries about real estate. For a brief moment, I had this fantasy that I could live in Del Mar and set up a consulting company for book publishers working from Del Mar. Like most such fantasies, I forgot all about it as soon as I returned to Manhattan.

No sooner had I returned than I received a call from the head of a small educational training company that wanted me to help them create some educational learning tapes about Southeast Asia. In my anthropological studies, I had worked with some fellow graduate students who were from Southeast Asia, or had done anthropological fieldwork there. In both cases, many slides were available. I was enjoying working on this project and thinking that there might be an opportunity to create my own consulting/content company. I hadn't incorporated yet, but I already had a name. When it had come time to pay me for the consulting work on the future of Arco, Jerry had handed me a form to fill out and asked me to come up with a name, since they could pay a company but not an individual. I had hesitated and not known what to write. Jerry suggested that I fill in the other parts of the form, including the mailing address. I was living at Waterside Plaza in Manhattan at the time, and by mistake, I wrote Waterside under the line for the name of the company. Jerry was going to hand me another form, but by then I had already filled out the rest of it correctly and said, "Never mind," and went ahead and added the word "Associates" after the first Waterside. Now, although I had no one to associate with and no employees, I was officially Waterside Associates.

With the success of my report on Arco, which led to a special presentation to Mr. Warnocke, Mr. Shaffer, and Mr. Grenquist (the brain trust of Prentice Hall Publishing at that time), it seemed as though I might actually be able to make a go of it as a publishing consultant under the rubric Waterside Associates. I will never forget the lunch I had with Mr. Warnocke, the chairman of the Board of Prentice Hall Publishing at that time. There I was, basically a kid in my twenties, with an opportunity to ask one of the most powerful and learned publishing executives anything I wanted to know about publishing. I had recently seen the Dustin Hoffman film *The Graduate,* so in my best imitation I asked Mr. Warnocke, "If there were one key piece of advice you would give to someone in publishing, what would it be?" The one word answer came back, "Distribution." I heard the word and returned a puzzled expression, waiting for the punch line. "Distribution is the single most important ingredient to publishing success. Never publish a book unless you know you already have distribution. It doesn't matter how good your product is unless you have distribution." Seemingly simplistic, this sound advice is still worth remembering.

The one problem I was having at Waterside Associates was figuring out where it might be leading me. I did not seem to have trouble getting consulting contracts, but I seemed limited by the amount of time I could spend on each project. There seemed no clear growth pattern for what was a thriving, if very much cottage industry type operation that was functioning from the kitchen table in my one bedroom Waterside Plaza apartment. I was discussing this dilemma with my younger brother, when he suggested that I call Peter Jovanovich. He had heard that Peter was teamed up with Chris Morris, an editor who had worked with him while he was running Macmillan trade books, and that Peter and Chris were serving as consultants and book packagers. I had gone to school with Peter in the seventh and eighth grades and respected him, since he usually managed to get things done in a consistent and orderly way. Hoping to learn a little something about how to set up a long-term business as a publishing consultant, I gave Peter a call. He suggested that we have lunch the following week, and gave me a number to call to confirm the lunch. Peter was doing some consulting for his father's firm, Harcourt Brace Jovanovich Publishing, and had access to a secretary at Harcourt who was keeping track of his appointments.

The following week, on the day of the scheduled lunch, I received a call from Peter's secretary. "Mr. Gladstone, I am so sorry, but Mr. Jovanovich is unable to keep his lunch date with you. Can we schedule for next Wednesday?" "Certainly," I replied, not overly concerned with the delay, since it was merely intended as an opportunity to gather information anyway.

Well, the Monday before the rescheduled lunch, I received my copy of *Publisher's Weekly,* the industry trade magazine for the book publishing industry. The lead article was about how William Jovanovich had just sacked seven editors the Friday before, and promoted Peter as a consultant to head the trade division of Harcourt Brace Jovanovich. Suddenly, my meeting with Peter had added significance. Peter was now in a position where he might be able to generate some consulting contracts, rather than just advice. Even though I had known Peter my whole adult life, I had had very little contact with him since about the tenth grade. Our lunch went smoothly, and we hardly talked about book publishing at all until the end of lunch. I remember Peter was extremely interested in what was happening with the computer industry, and how it might impact book publishing. I was firm in my belief that whatever happened with electronic forms of communication, there would always be a place for regular, paper-printed books. I suggested that there would probably be more books published as a result of the computer industry, rather than fewer. Peter agreed, and then took the conversation in a direction that I had never anticipated.

"Bill, my dad's decided that it's time to broaden the company's horizons. He's setting up an operation in San Diego, California, and wants to establish a trade division out there. Here in New York, everyone talks to the same agents about the same ideas. He feels that there are some fresh authors out there in California with ideas about self-help, real estate books, and other topics that we aren't seeing from the agents here in New York. We're looking for someone with an entrepreneurial background who also knows books."

"Well, I know books," I responded rather automatically.

"Well, would you be interested in the position?" came Peter's effortless suggestion.

"Well, I actually visited the Harcourt offices several months back, and spent some time up in Del Mar. The offices are really nice and I liked the area."

"Well, let me check with the Chairman [Peter's dad], and I'll get back to you."

"OK, but you should understand that I probably would only stay for two to three years. I view myself as an entrepreneur, and will eventually want to have my own company. I certainly need a couple of years of seasoning, but as long as two to three years would be enough to get the San Diego operation going, this could be quite interesting for me."

Peter seemed to ignore these last cautionary remarks as we got up from the table and moved toward the door. The next week went by and I heard nothing. I assumed that Peter didn't really have the authority to hire someone, or that his father hadn't approved of the idea of placing a relatively inexperienced editor in charge of his new San Diego operation. At that time I was still receiving mail at the Arco publishing offices, and would go down there once a week to gather my mail. As I walked in, my former secretary looked up and breathlessly called, "Mr. Gladstone, Peter Jovanovich's office has been trying to get a hold of you desperately for two days. There must be something wrong with your home phone. Here, call her right away. It seems to be very important."

"This is Bill Gladstone calling. Is Peter in?"

"Yes, just a moment."

"Bill, here's the deal. Your salary will be $35,000 to start. We'll give you a $10,000 signing bonus and cover your costs to move you out to San Diego. You'll be senior editor in charge of the San Diego operation, and will have an initial acquisition budget of $300,000 to acquire manuscripts. Within our normal royalty parameters, you can call your own shots. You'll report directly to me here in New York. Do you want the job?"

"Sounds good. Yes, I'll take it," I replied somewhat stunned, but also delighted, since this was an incredible opportunity for someone who had really rather limited experience with general interest rather than specialty books.

"Good. You need to be approved by the sales manager, Frank McCormick, who is already out there in San Diego. Frank used to work with me as the sales manager at Macmillan. I'm sure you'll get along. He'd like to meet with you on Friday in San Diego, and the Chairman will be in San Diego as well." Peter always referred to his father as "the Chairman," since William Jovanovich was the chairman of the board of Harcourt Brace Jovanovich, and this seemed more dignified than "Dad," or confusing matters with two Mr. Jovanovichs.

I made my own plane reservations, and, with some trepidation, showed up on Friday morning on the 11th floor of the former San Diego Athletic building, which now headquartered Harcourt's West Coast divisions. This included significant parts of the college division and Academic Press, as well as the incipient trade division.

When I arrived, I was greeted by an attractive and extremely pleasant young blonde woman who could not have been more than twenty-one years old. She introduced herself as Debbie, and informed me that Mr. McCormick was in a meeting with the Chairman and would not be available for at least another half an hour. She apologized on his behalf, but just the way she said "Chairman," it was obvious that Mr. Jovanovich senior was an imposing presence to whom schedules of underlings or would-be employees were not particularly significant.

Well, during that half hour I was rehearsing my responses and wondering if the chairman himself would be interviewing me as well. By this point, I had convinced myself that being senior editor at Harcourt and living in sunny California away from the congestion in New York City was definitely something I desired. I was no longer as calm and emotion free as I had been when I first went to lunch with Peter, not having a clue that a job opportunity might result from a casual lunch with an old friend.

It was already lunchtime by the time Mr. McCormick appeared from the inner sanctum. (The Chairman kept a private apartment on the eleventh floor of the San Diego building so that he would not need a hotel when visiting. He also had a lock on the elevator so that no one could enter the 11th floor without being accompanied by the security guard. Because of Mr. Jovanovich's rather flamboyant and sometimes hard line with employees and others, there had been numerous threats on his life. One of the most publicized had been an attempt by a disgruntled author to fly into the Harcourt building in New York directly on line with the Chairman's desk.) Frank invited me into his office, handed me a newspaper with some potential condos available for rent already circled, and suggested that the best place to live would be the North County along the beach in either Del Mar or Solana Beach, where he had chosen. "There's very little traffic out here, and you can make it to the office in less than twenty minutes. I think you'll like it," Frank opined.

I thanked Frank for the advice and started to sit down, thinking that I would now be interviewed for the job. Frank looked at his watch and gestured to the door. "Meyer the buyer is here from Harcourt's law books subsidiary and is joining us for lunch. Peter and Meyer are probably already over there, so we better get going."

Next thing I knew, I was sitting at lunch next to a gentleman in his early sixties named Meyer Fisher. Meyer had recently sold his company to Harcourt, and though he was still running that company, he was now also a special consultant to the Chairman on acquisitions and new ventures. Meyer had been called down to San Diego (for the meeting that had kept me cooling my heels) to discuss the formation of Books For Professionals, a new division that would compete with Arco and Shaum's in the self-help, test prep, and study guide book publishing fields. Frank had just been made sales manager and president of this division, and the Chairman had just appointed me founding editor. This was not actually clear to me during that lunch, which focused almost exclusively on the issue of whether or not to sign up a book that would contain drawings of the racecar drivers of the next running of the Indianapolis 500, which was scheduled to take place within the next two weeks. Apparently, Meyer had a young female protégé, who was also an artist, who proposed creating such a book. Meyer was all enthusiastic about the special sales potential of the book, and how it could be sold to car companies, oil companies, the fan clubs of different drivers, etc., etc. Frank was concerned about how many drawings, the size of the book, and how many copies he would have to sell through normal retail channels. During the conversation, Peter turned to me and said, "So, Bill, what do you think? Should we sign this book or not?" I had not seen a single piece of paper or drawing on this project, but the idea of this book sounded dubious to me. I could see that Meyer was really keen on the project and that Frank was not. Someone had to make a decision, and Peter did not seem particularly keen to alienate either party.

"Well, this is a hard one to call, but why don't you give the artist an option of two or three thousand dollars to be held against the advance, so that she can go out to Indianapolis and do some sample drawings. Then when she gets back, we can look at what she's done, gather some information on how likely the special sales really will be, and make a final decision then."

Everyone seemed pleased with this suggestion, and as we got up from lunch, Peter shook my hand and said "Congratulations," while Meyer inquired if I needed a ride back to the LA airport. I was pleased, but I was also disappointed. I had flown over three thousand miles to be interviewed for a job, and even though I already had the job, I wanted to be interviewed. I told Meyer that I would appreciate the ride, but that I needed about fifteen minutes to talk over some ideas with Frank. I actually only spent about five minutes with Frank, and didn't really get a chance to talk much about the operation that I was agreeing to start in San Diego, but at least it gave me the illusion of having received the interview that I had flown so far to have. In those five minutes, the only topic of substance was again Meyer's racing car book. Frank shared his view that "Meyer is always selling something. What a terrible idea for a book."

On the ride up to LA, Meyer filled me in on the real plans and motivations behind my hiring. Meyer had known my dad and had encouraged the Chairman to purchase Arco several years previously. Now that the company had been sold to Prentice Hall, it was no longer possible to buy it. When the Chairman had heard that I was meeting with Peter, he had immediately told Peter to hire me. The plan was to create the Books for Professionals publishing unit and compete directly with Arco. The Chairman figured that by having me on board he was getting the brain trust without the expense of buying an entire company. He was going to let me do trade books, but his clear agenda was utilizing my expertise in the self-help and test prep areas. Learning this did not greatly alter my enthusiasm for the position, because my bosses were still going to be more than 3,000 miles away, and I had signed a noncompete agreement with Prentice Hall when I left Arco that I assumed would insulate me somewhat from having to spend too much time with the test prep side of the business, which although profitable, was not nearly as exciting as the general books.

As we drove up the freeways, Meyer asked me what I thought of Peter and Frank. I was quite diplomatic, and offered that they both seemed to know what they were doing.

"Well, they are pretty good, but you're the heavy." "What do you mean?" I questioned. "Well, Peter and Frank are pretty good executives, but you're the one who we're counting on. You have real vision."

I was truly puzzled why Meyer thought this after a single luncheon together. My immediate thought was that since I was the only person who was semi-enthusiastic about his idea for the racing car book, that he was just flattering me. In retrospect, I think that Meyer really did see something in me that I did not see in myself. I remember him going on about how I was really great about packaging ideas and concepts. I wasn't even sure at the time what he was referring to. It took several years of publishing and hundreds of deals of my own later before I began to appreciate my own qualities that Meyer saw in those first few minutes.

Lessons to Be Learned:

(1) The second time around is rarely as exciting as the first.

(2) If going on a long trip to inaccessible places, it is probably a good idea to arrange some way of checking in with your home or home office.

(3) Anger is rarely a productive way of reacting to situations.

(4) Don't put too much trust into any individual or set of circumstances. Even one's own father may have a prior agenda that could disappoint you.

(5) No matter how potentially glamorous or lucrative, never take any assignment that in any way jeopardizes your integrity or breaks the law.

(6) If people want you to help them, do your best to help them, even if you see no clear and immediate gain for yourself.

(7) Make things as easy for yourself as possible. Whether this involves filling out a form, accepting a job, or being interviewed, just follow the path of least resistance and do what seems most genuine in the moment.

(8) Try to stay emotionally detached from any specific goal. One of the reasons my initial lunch meeting with Peter went so well was that I was not even aware that Peter had a job to offer me. One of the reasons the lunch in San Diego went so well was that I had no idea who Meyer Fischer was and gave advice not based upon trying to please anyone, but what (without the benefit of any real information) was a logical way to gather more information without committing the use of significant resources.

(9) Do not be intimidated by anyone, and do not be afraid to ask questions. The more senior an executive, the more likely they are to enjoy sharing knowledge. Be discrete, and don't presume on their time in the process.

(10) Don't limit yourself. You may not even be aware of your own gifts. If others see them, don't resist. Sometimes others can see you more objectively than you can see yourself.

(11) Do not agonize over your mistakes or misfortunes. I did go through a grieving period at the loss of Arco. I also, on more than one occasion, thought that my act of hubris in tearing up a guaranteed contract with Prentice Hall was probably an act of folly. But I did not dwell on those mistakes, and somehow it turned out that that error led to a position far superior to what I would have pursued at Arco.

(12) Be spontaneous and open to the magic in your life. Friendships dictated much of the sequence of landing the job with Harcourt, starting with the dinner in New York with Miguel Sanchez. I went to Del Mar and enjoyed the location. When Peter Jovanovich offered the position, I had already decided that I would be willing to move. Was it just luck that this sequence of events occurred? Of course, it was, and yet hadn't I somehow participated in creating that luck? The cynic could look at all the events and conclude that all it was really about was William Jovanovich seeing an opportunity to start a test prep division and my being his convenient pawn. There may be a level on which that is

what occurred, but there is also a level on which I subconsciously orchestrated the entire series of events, and I did so not by planning and scheming, but by allowing the natural flow of events to unfold, including my emotional response to the sale of Arco. My willingness to take risks and not resist opportunities offered to me while exploring my true desires allowed this good luck to evolve.

Key Insight:
APPLICATION

Cultivate the practice of applying your aptitudes with a positive attitude in all circumstances. Hard work when you love what you do is not hard.

CHAPTER 8

MY BRILLIANT CAREER PHASE TWO: MY MORNINGS AT HARCOURT. GAINFULLY EMPLOYED BUT NOT FOR LONG

Being in the Wrong Place at the Wrong Time

The first two weeks on the job, I reported to the Harcourt offices in New York City. I needed two weeks to get out of my lease and arrange for the move to California. One of the first calls I made was to my friend Bill Ury, who had been one of my fellow graduate students at Harvard. Bill was working on a book project with Roger Fisher, a law professor and head of the Harvard Negotiation project. The title of the book was *Getting to Yes.*

I asked Bill if the book were under contract to a publisher yet and was told that there was an offer from Houghton Mifflin, but that no contract had been signed. I immediately arranged to fly up to Cambridge to meet with Bill and Roger. Roger was the primary author and decision-maker, and although he was gracious, he explained that since it was practically my first day on the job and the competing editor was the editor-in-chief of Houghton Mifflin (and was also John Galbraith's editor), Harcourt would have to at least triple the $15,000 advance offer on the table if he were going to go with a neophyte, compared with a man of proven success and a shelf full of successful books to his credit.

I asked if there were a figure at which he would agree to sign without going back to Houghton Mifflin, as I wanted to avoid a bidding war. He said, "Yes. If you offer us $50,000, we'll take it." "OK, let me think about it, and I'll call you tomorrow," was my reply.

I had literally been on the job only two days and already had a major decision to make. Although Houghton was only offering $15,000, I believed in the book and figured it was worth the $50,000 they wanted. At the same time, $50,000 represented one-sixth of my first year's acquisition budget, and there would be 363 days left in the year.

When I went into the office the next day, I decided that the prudent thing to do would be to check with Frank McCormick. Frank was in town for a sales conference, and advised me to check with Peter, but his recommendation was to offer $25,000. I explained that I didn't think that would work, since I was sure Houghton would match $25,000, and we would probably lose the book. "Well, see what Peter thinks," was Frank's response.

I walked into Peter's office and explained the situation. I told him that I thought that Roger Fischer did not want to haggle and that he had been quite clear that for $50,000 he would abandon his greater psychological security of working with Houghton, but that if we offered less, we would risk alienating him altogether. Peter was more cynical than I about Fisher's position, and agreed with Frank. "Offer him $25,000 and see what happens," was his suggestion.

I offered $25,000, and Houghton matched that. True to his word, Mr. Fischer did not let me make another offer. He did not want to engage in a bidding war, and felt that it was awkward socially for him not to sign with his friend at Houghton Mifflin anyway and only a significant, three times plus price differential would be a graceful enough excuse.

In hindsight, I didn't fault myself too much for letting this book slip away. Given the no returns policy that Harcourt instituted later that year, which severely reduced any book's chance of becoming a bestseller, I remain pleased for my friend Bill that they did sign with Houghton, since under their publishing program the book went on to become a major bestseller with literally millions of copies now in print. At the same time, I also recognize that this was a major blunder. I let a book that was worth tens of millions of dollars slip away because I didn't have strong enough faith in my own judgment. I knew that the book was a good one and that the authors would do a great job promoting a title that had a large and clearly defined audience, and yet instead of just going with my gut and risking it, I wanted the security of consensus from my marketing manager and my boss. It was not their job to make this call—it was mine and I blew it. What I have told all editors from this experience is, "If they give you the dice, roll them, or they'll get another player." This was one of the few times that I allowed insecurity to enter into a negotiation, and I offer this example as how not to "be the deal." Committee decisions are seldom strong decisions. You have to feel with your gut the value of a deal and stay with that feeling. If you are wrong, OK, you might blow it, but at least you will have blown it or succeeded on the strength of your own convictions and not those of a committee. The worst that can happen if you blow it is that you will be fired, but at least you will have been a player. You can only really lose if you fail to play at all.

At the time we lost the chance to publish *Getting to Yes*, there was no way of knowing that the book was going to become a number one bestseller, and the consensus from Peter and Frank was that it was probably just as well that we didn't get the book. The next week I was off to San Diego, and the fun really began.

My first assignment was to represent the company at the Santa Barbara's writer's conference. This is one of the most established and best settings of any of the major writing conferences. Swifty Lazar was in attendance that year, as well as Ray Bradbury and many other luminaries. Among them was Werner Erhard of EST fame. Mr. Erhard's book about his technique had been a number one bestseller, and he was invited to talk to the writers about the art of writing. Given the nature of his book and the fact that a ghostwriter had actually written most of it, this seemed an odd choice of topics. Erhard was terrible, and many of the writers were livid at his meandering talk, which showed a complete lack of empathy or understanding with the plight of a real writer. He offered one valuable insight, which was to "write from your own experience," as well as some great suggestions about how to promote your book if you already have a national reputation and a staff of fifty or more behind you.

I was scheduled to give a talk immediately after Erhard's speech in a much smaller room, and toward the end of my talk, there were several questions, some of them about Erhard's just-completed talk. I was candid, as is my style, and answered the question with my typical bluntness, opining that "the talk was basically worthless."

Unbeknownst to me, Mr. Erhard himself, together with a few of his entourage, had entered the conference room toward the end of my talk. I had not noticed when they first entered, but I did notice Erhard now. I was sure that he was going to speak up and defend his speech, but instead he just stared at me in total shock and disbelief. There were several more questions relating to the Erhard speech, some by his group of almost fifty (who seemed to accompany him everywhere), designed to provoke or embarrass me into a retraction. I held my ground and just stated and restated my opinion in specific terms as to why many of the arguments of the Erhard speech were so vacuous. I was not trying to embarrass Mr. Erhard, but I was not going to withdraw my sincere opinions just to be polite.

At the end of the talk, I was feeling rather sheepish. I had not intended to offend the special guest speaker of the conference or insult him, but I knew I had. My belief later was that the only reason Mr. Erhard did not speak up himself was that he had been surrounded by handlers and sycophants and "yes people" for so long that he had no objectivity about his own shortcomings. He was so used to people being enamored of his every phrase that to have someone criticize him so directly must have been a totally unique and shocking experience.

Much to my surprise, the next morning when I went to breakfast, I received a standing ovation from the several hundred writers
gathered at the tables. Mr. Erhard had already left for his next semi-
nar, so people were able to show their appreciation without offending him. Word had spread of how I had confronted Mr. Erhard with
what the majority of the writers felt was the truth, and there was
sincere relief that the pabulum being passed by Mr. Erhard the evening before had not been allowed to pass unchallenged.

The rest of the conference was pretty much a blur, though I
did end up meeting Willow and Dusk Weaver, which eventually led
to the publication of their esoteric account of homesteading and
seeking a serene life in harmony with nature. This book was one of
my two allotted non-commercial efforts allowed as a discretionary
book over the protests of Frank McCormick. The book never did
make any money nor in the end was it ever published by Harcourt
at all, but the Weavers had high integrity and that was what I was
looking for.

As for the daily routine back in San Diego, it turned out to be
better than I could have ever imagined. Frank and I would get into
the office around ten, since if we got in any earlier we would be
missing the New York people, who would be going to lunch anyway.
We would work a couple of hours and then go to lunch. By the time
we returned to our desks at two P.M., the New York people were starting to leave. By three P.M., Frank and I usually would call it a day.

Despite these better-than-banker's hours, we were extremely
productive. We didn't have to go to any meetings, and there were no
committees. Other than the folks in New York, there was nobody to
talk to except Debbie Warren, our shared secretary. The day would
start with me going through the fifty or sixty proposals and manuscripts that would arrive daily. I would quickly skim the first page or
so of each, and if I saw a topic that caught my eye, I would put it in
the possible pile. The others went straight to the reject pile. Out of
fifty, perhaps five would make it to the "possible" pile. I would spend
another ten to fifteen minutes with each of these possibles. By then
it would be close to twelve, and I would go into Frank's office and

ask him, based upon the topic and the author's credentials, how many copies of each possible book he would be able to sell if the book were extremely well written and well edited. In most cases, Frank would say none or 5000 or some other small number, and the possible would become a reject. If and only if Frank thought we might be able to sell 25,000 or more copies would I then take the manuscript home and actually read it. Only one or two possibles a week made it into this category, so I did not feel overworked. Despite this, I signed up about twenty books in the first six months, and was way ahead of schedule in making up for the seven editors sacked just before I was hired. I was promised my own assistant, but there ended up being a hiring moratorium, and I never was able to hire anyone else. This was unfortunate not so much for the trade side of the business, but for the test prep side, where we ended up having to rely on New York production staff, some of whom were less than reliable.

The way the test prep side of the business was jump-started is a story in itself. It was perhaps the second month of my tenure when Frank buzzed me on the intercom. "I've got a woman on the phone who is talking a mile a minute. I don't understand a word she is saying, but if she knows half the people whose names she is dropping, she is probably worth talking to." I also found this voice to be amazingly breathless in trying to squeeze a hundred minutes' worth of ideas into a two-minute conversation. She ended her final sentence with, "Can I come in to see you?" and considering I didn't have any lunch plans for the day, I said, "Sure, come on in." Well, this was probably a mistake, but it led to one of the stranger encounters in my publishing life.

Glenda Finn was an unusual woman. She walked into my office, looked at me, and started to tell me her story. She was accompanied by a gentleman who was going to be her ghostwriter, and who also had his own book about Tesla that he was pitching, as well as a second book about UFOs. This was all a bit too flakey for a Yale and Harvard trained anthropologist, even if I had participated in the filming of *In Search of Ancient Mysteries*. Glenda's own story was incredible. She had been pregnant with her first child and had been in an elevator accident that resulted in her going into a coma and hemorrhaging. She was rushed to the emergency room, where her seven-month old fetus was delivered successfully. Glenda herself, however, took a turn for the worse. The doctors could not diagnose what was wrong as her vital signs started to give out. According to her, while in a coma she drifted through a white tunnel toward a place of peace. It was explained to her that she was dying of blood poisoning, because she had actually been carrying twins, and the afterbirth of the second twin was poisoning her. I did not have the medical background to know if this were possible, but the next part of her story was even more outrageous. In a brief moment of lucidity, she regained consciousness out of her coma and told the doctors in attendance exactly what she had been told, that it was necessary to remove the afterbirth and she would recover. According to Glenda, the doctors did this and she survived.

Unfortunately for Glenda, while in this life/death state she was given the names of certain individuals, as well as some clairvoyant abilities. Although she tried to return to the life of a normal house-wife from a family of good breeding, she was obsessed with follow-ing up on these twelve names and discovering why they had been given to her. One of them was Paul Brenner, a doctor in San Diego, who was also a writer with whom I was in discussions concerning his own book. That coincidence aside, I did not think that this story was one that Harcourt, which had hired me to publish highly com-mercial nonfiction, would be interested in, and was ready to politely terminate the interview, when Glenda started describing a vision of a diagram that had been in a dream the night before. The diagram she described was contained in the first book I had written for Arco many years before, and was now out of print: *How to Score High on the Medical College Admission Test.* She next described seven pieces of colored silk in a drawer. Again, I was shocked. Through an odd set of circumstances, seven such colored pieces of silk had come into my possession while filming in India, and were residing in a drawer in my condo. My skepticism was starting to fade, but then Glenda

86

told me that the Chairman was going to be sending for me to go to New York within the next two weeks and that within two years I would have my own company, and no longer be working directly with Frank and Peter Jovanovich. I thought this highly unlikely, at least the part about the Chairman asking me to fly to New York, since I had just been in New York and there was no pending project that would require my presence. I still did not see a way of publishing Glenda's book, but I was definitely intrigued. I was even more startled two days later when I received a call from the Chairman asking me to get on a plane so that I could be in the New York conference room at ten A.M. to discuss a major new opportunity.

That new opportunity turned out to be the purchase of the Monarch test prep line from Simon & Schuster. The Chairman kept Peter, Frank, Meyer (the buyer) Fischer, who had brought this deal to the Chairman's attention, and myself waiting for over an hour. We had all flown in (except Peter) the day before on the private corporate jet from California just to discuss the opportunity. The Chairman finally showed up, sat down, and gave a brief five-minute monologue on why he thought we should pursue this purchase. He asked for opinions, and I immediately suggested that it would be more cost effective and we would have better quality books if we just developed our own titles. The Chairman expressed his view that time to market might be worth the extra money. I countered that it was a very crowded field and that it might not be the best time to enter the test prep arena. The Chairman countered that there were two ideal times to enter a market: "When no one is in a market and when everyone is in a market." I found this rather cryptic, but interpreted it to mean that the only time to avoid a market opportunity is when there are just a few modest established players, with no one making any real money. In any event, I was not eager to have Harcourt pursue this opportunity, since it was obvious that I would be burdened with overseeing the editorial side of the operation, and if I weren't going to be an owner of Arco, I had vowed that I wasn't going to edit test prep books for a living. I mentioned to the Chairman that he should take into consideration that I had a noncompete with Prentice Hall that prevented me from working on test prep books for a period of three years. I (not Prentice Hall) had actually insisted on this noncompete, since I consciously knew that someone might want me to do test prep books, and my desire was nil. The Chairman just winked when I mentioned the noncompete and said, "Don't worry about that. That's why we have lawyers."

The next thing we knew, the Chairman was looking at his watch as he stood up and declared, "Well gentlemen, I have another meeting to attend, so the decision is in your court. Just be sure that Meyer gets a vote. I'm sure that you'll make the right decision," and with a flourish, he was gone, back to his private office.

Well, there it was. After flying all of us six hours or more to his meeting and keeping us waiting, after less than ten minutes the Chairman disappears, leaving the illusion that we have something to meet about. We chatted for about another five minutes, but it was obvious that the decision to purchase had already been made, and we were really there just to ratify the decision and accept the fact that I would have to edit and produce these books and that Frank would have to find a way to sell these books. We discussed a few details relating to a salesperson that came with the deal, and the process whereby the manuscripts would be sent to me for review, and adjourned for lunch. Glenda Finn had been right on her first prediction, and I was beginning to wonder about her other prognostications as well.

The rest of that first year passed relatively uneventfully. I continued to give speeches and meet with authors and sign books. The established book authors in San Diego were so delighted to have an opportunity to meet with a real live book editor that despite publishing protocol they were insisting on buying me lunch just to show their gratitude of having a publishing professional to discuss their book ideas with them in an intelligent manner. I also took to setting up meetings with the heads of other book divisions, including college and the magazine groups, to discuss joint ventures with my trade division. I did this partially because I was extremely naive, and had read in a report from the annual meeting that the

Chairman had mentioned that he had just hired a brilliant young editor (me) who was going to explore the synergistic opportunities between divisions. The Chairman had never informed me that this was his agenda, but I assumed that the speech was indicative of what he assumed I would do. In retrospect, I now understand that "synergy" was just the buzzword of the moment and that he really didn't care if I tried to organize cross-divisional projects or not. Unfortunately, the heads of the other divisions did care. They were decidedly against it. There was so much political positioning at the company, with each division carefully guarding their own turf and bottom line to protect not only salary increases and bonuses, but also opportunities for advancement. No one wanted to have a single dime of their resources or any of their manpower extended on any project that did not directly benefit their bottom line. I never cared about who got credit, but the nature of the projects I suggested to other division heads usually involved repurposing their material for trade books. I would offer a share of revenues to go to their divisions, but this did not seem to appease them. They assumed that since my office was next to the Chairman's in San Diego, that I was just promoting these projects as a way of currying favor with the chairman. This was never my motivation, but I alienated other executives nonetheless. This came back to haunt me in an unexpected development that eventually led to my dismissal.

Before exploring those circumstances in greater depth, I should comment on the one big fish that got away under my tenure in San Diego. I received a visit from an author named Spencer Johnson, who had a proposal for a book he was calling *The One Minute Scolding*. Spencer was a former MD who had turned to writing. He had created *The Value Tales* with his wife for a small press, and he fashioned himself a writer. He had since been divorced and fallen on hard times. After the divorce, he was having discipline problems with his children and had been fortunate enough to meet the Del Mar psychiatrist, Gerald Nelson. Dr. Nelson had a technique for disciplining children combining shaming with praising. He called the technique "the one minute scolding." Dr. Nelson was not a writer, and since Spencer presented himself as a writer, he convinced Dr. Nelson that they should co-author a book together based upon this technique. Spencer had written up a first draft of the proposed book, and although it needed significant revision, I saw immediately that this was a great idea. Frank thought he could sell at least twenty-five thousand copies, so I offered Spencer a thirty-five thousand dollar advance. Spencer wanted more, but I explained that we were anticipating an initial lay down of 25,000 books and that we needed to sell more than that even to justify the $35,000 advance. "Besides," I told him, "you'll make more in royalties, because this book will sell for a long time." Spencer said he understood, and told us to send him the contract.

After receiving the contract, Spencer called back and negotiated a few additional changes that were relatively insignificant, and said that he would be by the next day to return the contract. I invited Spencer to lunch, expecting to have the contracts returned. Spencer did not indicate any problems throughout the meal, and I started to explain to him the direction that I wanted him to take in revising the manuscript. Toward the end of the meal, I mentioned that one of the great things about *The One Minute Scolding* was that the technique lent itself to the development of a full series. You could apply the principle to management, teaching and other fields. Spencer's eyes lit up as he realized that this would be much more than a single book deal.

After the meal, I asked Spencer for the contracts. He apologized and said that he had rushed out of the house to make the lunch meeting, and had left the contracts on the kitchen table. He would mail them to us that day. I wished him well, and noticed that he had a hole in his sports jacket, and wondered if he were financially stable enough to get the book done before the advance arrived. I waited a week and there was no contract. I called Spencer. Only his answering machine responded. I left a message. Still no contract. I waited another week. I called Spencer again. When I finally got him on the phone, Spencer said that he had decided not to sign the contract. I called his coauthor, Dr. Nelson, and Dr. Nelson did not have an explanation other than that Spencer had called him as well, and told him that he wanted to shelf the project. Apparently, Spencer had taken the contract to his bank and arranged a loan on the basis of the contract. He later teamed up with Ken Blanchard and created The One Minute Manager, which became a phenomenal bestseller. I never thought much of Spencer as a writer, but he was a phenomenal promoter, and he showed true business genius in teaming up with Ken Blanchard, the ideal co-author for *The One Minute Manager.*

Other publishing executives have often asked me what I thought of Spencer, and although I think his ethics were deplorable, I admired his ability to execute. I may have had the original idea for The One Minute Manager, but the key is execution, not the idea alone. I tell authors this when they are worried about protecting an idea. I tell them that you can't and that your ability to execute quickly and well is your only real protection. I did learn from the experience, and as Peter Jovanovich later scolded me, "Don't ever do any editorial analysis, or at least don't share that analysis with an author until you have a signed contract. Authors aren't to be trusted." Of course, some authors are to be trusted, but this is not a bad general rule in publishing if one is concerned about protecting their efforts.

The biggest single issue during my tenure at Harcourt was the controversial attempt of the Chairman to single-handedly reverse the returns policy, which for decades has been the bane of a publisher's existence. Basically, all books are sold by publishers to bookstores on a consignment basis. Bookstores are billed for all books shipped, but they have the right to return any books that don't sell. As a result, it is difficult for a publisher to accurately project the right number of books to print and sell. The salespeople earn money based on commission, which is based on the number of books they sell, so they are pushing books like crazy. The booksellers prefer to only order as many books as they logically think they can sell, but there is no major penalty for over-ordering. The result is chaos and bad margins for book publishers. The elimination of the returns policy would be extremely beneficial to book publishers, and the Chairman decided that he would just do away with the returns policy single-handedly, and hoped that the rest of the industry would follow.

Well, all the rest of the industry did was follow the plight of Harcourt authors. Books that advanced 50,000 copies under the returns policy might only advance 10,000 now. That ratio of one to five pretty much held on every title. From the point of view of Frank as sales manager and myself as senior editor, this no-returns policy was not working. We were not encouraged to share our views with the Chairman or anyone else, but as much as we admired the courage of the initiative and wisdom of the goal, it was clear to us that the new policy was a disorder.

There was some irony here because indirectly my dad had been partly responsible for creating the returns policy in the first place. He had recounted his experiences in selling books to Macy's in the late 1930s. He was selling *Post Office Clerk Carrier,* and *Fireman Civil Service Exam* books, and they moved very nicely before a major test, but after a test they would just languish with no sales for up to six months until the next exam date. The book buyer at Macy's told Milton that he would not be ordering any more books because, even though they sold well initially, he would end up being stuck with unsaleable merchandise. My dad came up with the idea of allowing all the books to be returned after every major exam, since he would then immediately replace them with books for the next upcoming civil service examination. It was really more of a stock balancing plan the way it worked with test prep books than a true returns policy. Of course, once Macy's instituted this policy with Arco, they started pressing Simon & Schuster and the other major publishing houses for the same policy, although the categories of books did not make the transition as easy for the publishers. "Milt over at Arco can afford to take the books back, why can't you?" was the complaint from Macy's. Pretty soon, the other publishers matched the Arco returns policy, and a monster had been unleashed.

It was the Chairman's goal to re-leash this monster, and my job to loyally support this effort. We both failed, and we failed dramatically and publicly. The publicly part was the most problematic. It was always my opinion during those years that the Harcourt Trade Division existed more for prestige than for profit. The division published T. S. Eliot and many distinguished authors, and was used to publish Mr. Jovanovich's personal agenda of Eastern European intellectuals, who were fabulous writers but whose books never sold particularly large numbers. The division was a credit to book publishing, and had a wonderful Children's Books Division that not only won awards, but was profitable. On the other hand, Adult Trade, aside from the wonderful Helen Wolff line, always seemed to lack focus and direction. The division did, however, serve as wonderful PR for the School and College divisions and the professional academic books, which were much bigger and more significant to the company's overall bottom line, which was approaching one billion dollars in revenues during my short tenure in 1980 to 1981.

In my opinion, the fact that the no-returns policy accounted for an extra few million dollars in losses that year was probably not of any great significance to the Chairman. The fact that his policy was impractical and did not work did hurt his ego, however, and this was worse than losing money.

The beginning of the end started simply enough for me. I was interviewed by a local writer for *San Diego Magazine* and the magazine ended up deciding that the interview was worth a two-page spread in the magazine, with half of the first page a picture of me and the article primarily recounting my view of publishing in the West. I had not sought the interview, but since part of my job was to get the attention of agents and writers, I thought that a little publicity wouldn't be a bad thing. After all, the company was sending me to these writer's conferences to achieve the same goal—find material or have the material find me.

There had been another reporter trying for months to arrange an interview with me, and since he wrote for the local *Tribune* as a freelancer and had less on the ball than the *San Diego Magazine* writer, I continually put him off. He had called me on at least five different occasions, and when the *San Diego Magazine* article came out, he called me for a sixth time. I had really run out of excuses, and told him that he could come in the following day and we would have lunch. Well, the following day, I received a call from Fred Warshofsky, my buddy and former boss from the *In Search of Ancient Mysteries project*. Fred just happened to be in San Diego promoting his latest book and was available for lunch. I told him to come right over, forgetting until almost lunchtime that I had told the reporter to come in. I tried calling the reporter around 11 o'clock, but it was too late. He must have already left. The reporter showed up at about ten to twelve, and I explained to him that an author was coming, and I wouldn't be able to give him the interview after all. Fred walked in just as I was explaining this to the reporter, and Fred, feeling compassion for a fellow writer, offered, "Bill, we don't have anything of specific confidence to discuss. Why don't we invite him along?" I paused a second and then said, "OK, but just remember that anything you hear during lunch is off the record." The reporter just smiled and was so grateful that he was going to get to tag along.

During lunch, Fred started to complain about the latest advance I had offered him on his next book. It was only about half of what he had received on his previous book. I explained to Fred that the topic was somewhat speculative and that it didn't really matter in the long run because if we were successful with the book it would earn out, and he would make just as much in the long run in royalties. He protested that with a smaller advance, however, there was less likelihood that the company would market the book aggressively. I countered that that was not necessarily the case. When he challenged that assertion, to demonstrate my point, I offered the best-selling *Free to Choose* published by Harcourt two years previously, before the no-returns policy and still number one on the bestseller list. It had been publically reported in *Publisher's Weekly* that the book had been signed for no advance, so I did not feel it inappropriate to mention this fact to Fred as proof of the possibility of a book being hugely promoted even if the advance were small or non-existent.

I didn't think too much about that lunch or that conversation until the next day. It was only a two-inch column in *The San Diego Tribune,* but it was the catalyst for changing my life. The reporter was a man in his sixties who was only a stringer for the newspaper. He had been a writer for a manufacturing trade magazine and retired to San Diego. He didn't understand the rules of reporting and didn't know what off the record meant. He also didn't believe in checking his facts with his sources before having them published. I know that he was trying to create some positive publicity for me as gratitude for allowing him to come to lunch and giving him the opportunity to have something published to maintain his status as a stringer for the newspaper, since this modestly paying hobby was giving his later years some real meaning and purpose. In the article, it was presented as though I had been Milton Friedman's editor, and was directly responsible for this huge success. It was further pointed out that the savvy economist had opted for no advance so that he could receive a higher royalty. I had mentioned the higher royalty, but this was not higher than the top to which all contracts escalate after ten thousand copies, and I am sure that the lack of taking an advance was more due to tax considerations and his personal relationship with the Chairman (who had signed the book himself) than it had to do with any economic strategy on the part of Mr. Friedman. In any event, this short article was the final straw that ended my career at HBJ.

The head of the College Division had been particularly upset with the kind of publicity I was gaining, and had sent the *San Diego Magazine* article to the Chairman directly. He now clipped and sent this article with a little note inquiring if the Chairman was comfortable with this grandstanding young editor. I think his main axe with me was my ability to excite his editors about some of the trade projects that I saw coming out of their college authors—a useless distraction from his point of view. Timing is the key to business and my timing could not have been worse for gathering this kind of publicity. The Chairman had just announced that he was going to move all of Harcourt from New York to San Diego and Florida, and it did not look good to have a young editor running amuck getting credit for his own personal achievements, such as the signing of Milton Friedman's best-selling book *Free To Choose*. Mr. Jovanovich informed Peter that my presence was no longer required at the company.

The article had hit the San Diego papers on a Thursday. That Friday I had left the office early since a friend of mine from Spain, Antonio Villanueva, was visiting, and we had decided to go down to San Filipe for a fishing expedition. The fishing expedition was a great success, and using shrimp heads as bait, we caught more rock cod in four hours Saturday morning than we could ever eat, and instead gave them to the villagers for a fried fish taco extravaganza. We headed back to San Diego, where I learned that my girlfriend had decided that our relationship was over. This had me very much down in the dumps when I went to work on Monday.

Unknown to me, the article had been in the special pouch sent on Friday from San Diego that arrived every Monday to New York with the sales reports and any other vital pieces of information to be shown to the Chairman. The Chairman had seen the article at the equivalent of seven o'clock in the morning San Diego time. Knowing my schedule, Peter waited until ten o'clock San Diego time to give me a call.

"Bill, in the old country we would put you in the brig, but since this is civilian life, we can only take away your stripes. You have until Friday to clean out your desk. As they say in the army, loose lips sink ships. It is the Chairman's opinion that you betrayed confidences and confidential information and that you are being fired for breach of fiduciary responsibility. Frank and Debbie have already been informed. I can't really disagree with the Chairman about this." Well, for a moment. I thought about giving my side of the story and pointing out that nothing that was reported had not already been reported in the trade press, but I realized that it really didn't matter. I was really bummed out by the break-up of the relationship with my girlfriend the day before and was still in shock over that unexpected development. This was only an additional shock, not the biggest shock of the last twenty-four hours.

I sat in my office, relatively stunned, for the next hour or so. One of the reasons no one else had taken the Harcourt job in the first place was that this was a predictable event. William Jovanovich eventually fired anyone who made waves of any kind. He would let people work for him and give them all kinds of freedom in the beginning, but then slowly remove their autonomy and authority if they started to become too successful or go up against any of his own pet projects. I did not begrudge this approach of the Chairman because he was one of the most brilliant men ever to go into publishing. He had earned his success the hard way, starting with nothing as the son of immigrant coal workers and working his way from commission rep for Arco (ironically, his very first job in publishing was for my father), to sales rep for Harcourt, to eventually taking over all of Harcourt and leading it toward unprecedented heights.

As I tried to formulate a plan of action and truly understand what had just happened, the phone rang. It was Jeanette Gosney and that call generated the next chapter of my brilliant career and the creation of Waterside Productions.

Lessons to Be Learned:

(1) If they give you the dice, roll them.

(2) Pay attention to the unusual and do not completely ignore soothsayers.

(3) Be cautious with authors who fail to return contracts in a timely manner.

(4) Be cautious in talking to the press.

(5) Don't believe everything you hear.

(6) Ignore the interests of others at your own risk.

(7) Work smart, not hard; though be willing to work hard if necessary. (I did not recount in this chapter some very hard work I also did which involved taking two weeks off my daily

routine to hole up in my condo and personally rewrite our division's first big book when it was delivered as an unpublishable manuscript. The book was published successfully with great reviews.)

(8) Execution of a concept or idea is ultimately more important than an idea or concept itself.

(9) Resist destiny if you must, but if it persists, don't fight too hard. I did everything in my power to protect myself from having to work with test prep books. Yet even with a specially created noncompete, they came back to me.

(10) If you are going to be sacked, you might as well experience another major life crisis simultaneously, since it dulls the pain.

Key Insight:
ACCEPTANCE

Learn to accept the ups and downs and the major forces which are not under your control. Apply yourself as hard as you can to achieve your goals and dreams, but accept defeat if inevitable, and learn, through acceptance, to turn defeats into victories.

CHAPTER 9

MY BRILLIANT CAREER PHASE THREE: THE CREATION OF WATERSIDE

A Saga of Nonlinear Events

Jeanette Gosney was the wife of Michael Gosney. Michael was the owner of a small typesetting production company called The Word Company. Most of the revenue for The Word Company came from putting together newsletters for corporations and creating copy. Michael, with the help of Jeanette, had built a respectable business, with Jeanette responsible for doing the majority of the selling to magazines and other organizations and Michael in charge of the creative side of the business. Using the modest profits of the company, Michael had decided to launch Avant Books, a publishing company specializing in avant-garde literature and related nonfiction. Among his first titles were the play *Buddha* by Kozenzakis and *Deep Ecology* by Michael Tobias. There were about half a dozen titles under contract, and Jeanette was starting to see all of the profits from the Word division being squandered on books that, though receiving great reviews, were not selling particularly well.

Michael had called me soon after I arrived in San Diego, and I had taken an immediate liking to him. He did not have a college degree, and yet was intensely intellectual and artistic. He was a poet with a tremendous ambition to participate in the world of letters. I admired his ambition and resolve. I would take Michael to lunch once or twice a month and try to advise him on the publishing side of his business. I had met Jeanette at dinners and parties at their home, and I had remembered just two weeks previously when Jeanette had come to me privately at a party, and asked me if I could provide some serious consulting services to them. She was watching their finances and was becoming concerned. If something didn't change soon, they were headed for bankruptcy. I told her that I would be happy to help, but she said not just casually, but on a regular basis, perhaps one day a week and they would even try to pay me. I reassured her that I would come by and that it wouldn't be necessary to pay me. I would be delighted to help out.

Just minutes after being fired by Peter Jovanovich, I received a phone call from Jeanette Gosney, and I did not have my wits about me, but I saw no reason not to take her call. "Bill, Michael and I are here, and we would like to set up a time for you to come by and look at the books and help us reorganize. Can you give us a day this week?"

"Well, I could probably come down Saturday, but I think I can do even better than that. Starting Monday, why don't I come down every day? I'll help you guys out three days a week in exchange for use of an office and a secretary to work on my own business. I'm going to be leaving Harcourt in a few days, and I will need a place from which to launch my new company."

Well, this was an offer they couldn't refuse—a free editorial director/consultant for three days a week, without increasing their overhead. As soon as I hung up the phone, I got excited about the idea of starting my own company. My real ambition was to create a movie company based on my experiences with *In Search Of Ancient Mysteries,* and now I would have my opportunity. I had always envied Michael's opportunity to work on such interesting, if unprofitable books. Now I would be able to participate in a more active role. This was all a bit of wishful thinking, but it made the transition from senior editor to unemployed extremely smooth.

Those first few weeks were tough. Debbie and Frank commiserated and took me out at their own expense for one final dinner, since I was basically unpersoned by Harcourt. Based on the experience of other sacked employees, I felt I was treated with great respect. Instead of having a guard appear within five minutes of the phone call to watch over me as I emptied my desk and was escorted from the building (as was usual practice), I was given until Friday to clear out, and the security guard helped me carry my boxes, rather than just glaring, as might have been the case in New York. I always attributed the greater civility of my firing to the Chairman having worked for my father early on, and the relatively genuine affection that he seemed to have for me prior to the firing.

In any event, things looked pretty bleak, but at least I had a convivial place to go every morning, with interesting people and interesting projects. The problem was that none of them were making any money, nor were they likely to. We cut back and reorganized, and had Word Company focus more on the profit-generating projects, while taking the book expansion more slowly. On my own, I started working on a video project that seemed promising. I was able to make use of public access video equipment, and, on a shoestring budget, was producing what I thought would be the next great product. I finally met with the distributor after I had a rough-cut, and was told what they would pay, and how many they would take. Based on their bid, I would only lose about fifty cents on every video I sold. Perhaps I could make it up on volume, but this did not seem propitious.

As often happens when an editor leaves a publishing house, his or her book projects become orphans. There is no one in the publishing house who really cares about a project in the works once the editor is gone, unless it is from an established or highly commercial author. Since I had specialized in finding new and unproven talent, none of my projects were of great interest to those entrusted with following up. Two of these projects were cancelled, and the authors had not used agents, and were not sure how they should proceed. The first of these was *The Conquest of Cancer*, by Dr. Virginia

Livingston-Wheeler. Dr. Livingston was an amazing woman. She was in her seventies, but full of energy. She gave incredible parties at her home that included belly dancing, Broadway revues, and magnificent catered meals and entertainment. Dr. Livingston had been the first female intern in the New York City hospital system and had always done pioneering work. She established the Livingston Clinic in San Diego, which was a pioneer in alternative treatment modalities for cancer treatment and prevention. She had early on discovered the link between cancer and diet and had made many breakthrough discoveries that were controversial and challenged by the American Medical Association. In doing my research, I talked with numerous patients and discovered that she had had a remarkable success rate with dozens of patients pronounced terminal by traditional specialists. I was no doctor, but that was enough for me to feel that it was worth taking a chance on her and her book. My successor at HBJ did not share my enthusiasm and cancelled the contract request that I had put through shortly before I was sacked. The second project was by David Loye, and was entitled *The Sphinx and the Rainbow*. This was also a controversial book about the holographic theory of the nature of the universe and scientific evidence for the ability to predict the future. Dr. Loye presented an explanation that seemed worthy of print at a minimum and, based on my own experiences with Glenda Finn and the encounters of my parents regarding the crystal ball that foresaw the paper in Hawaii, deserved serious academic investigation as well. Not the opinion of the brain trust at Harcourt. Cancelled.

Both of these authors eventually called me to ask what could be done. I explained that they should not panic, that I had some friends in New York, and that I would help them out. I made a trip back to New York that spring to see if I could find someone to take on these books. It turned out that it was not easy to interest the editors. The Loye book required too much thinking and the Livingston book idea, though of interest, was really more of an idea than a complete book proposal. I went back to San Diego somewhat downhearted, but persevered. By then I had already incorporated my new company as Waterside Productions, Inc., anticipating great growth and success as a film company. I had also realized that, like it or not, I would also be doing some book agenting just to help out old friends. While at Avant Books, I would go through the mail to sort out book proposals. One of the query letters was from an established nonfiction author by the name of Ed Addeo. Ed was pitching a novel and included a list of his numerous successful collaborations on nonfiction books. I knew Avant was not in a position to take on any more novels, but I thought that Ed might have the ideal credentials to work with Dr. Livingston in order to turn her idea into a real book. Not knowing how Ed would react, I gave him a call. I asked Ed if he had ever heard of Dr. Virginia Livingston-Wheeler, and in one of those incredible coincidences that were becoming more and more common in my life, he got all excited and started raving about her. "I wrote an article about her once. She should win the Nobel Prize. I sent a terminally ill friend to her clinic, and she saved his life. She is just incredible. I would love to co-write a book with her about her clinic and her treatment program," enthused Ed. With Ed's talents, it did not take long to put together a really strong proposal. Off it went to New York, and the following September, I received a phone call and an offer, and I—after leaping what seemed like six feet into the air with joy— started to negotiate the deal. This was the first revenue-generating act I had engaged in since leaving Harcourt the previous November, and, though the commission was relatively paltry, it was one of the best feelings I ever had. Maybe I would be able to sustain myself after all and would not have to go back to New York with my tail between my legs, forced to admit that the idea of creating my own company with little or no resources and no plan was true folly, as my father suggested on more than one occasion. In his words, "There is nothing to prevent you from getting a real job. You really don't have to do this, you know."

But something inside of me really did have to do this, and the following week when a relatively obscure publisher at the time, Shambhala, called to purchase the David Loye book, I was beginning to feel almost solvent and took the huge step of leasing my own office space right in Del Mar. I didn't really lease my own space, but a single hundred square foot office with a desk in the law offices of an attorney friend of mine by the name of Carlo Coppo, who had his own literary interest and the empty space, which he was willing to rent to me for $350 a week. This $350 a week included access to the photocopier, the phone, and even use of his receptionist to answer my phone line. I negotiated to pay his legal secretary a dollar a page to type my correspondence.

I was now in business as a literary agency and started to look around for other projects. There were several unusual attributes to Waterside Productions, Inc. from the very beginning. First off, of course, was the fact that I never intended Waterside to be a literary agency in the first place. I wanted to concentrate on films and other special projects, but that just didn't seem to be in the cards initially. Despite my meager resources, I never considered a chapter S corporation. I decided right from the beginning that Waterside was going to be a major success and created a C corporation. I had this vision that Waterside would eventually encompass a number of spin-off corporations and that a C would be the best form to accomplish this over the long haul. I had to spend an extra thousand dollars or so to achieve this, and even though that was a significant percentage of my total reserves, I never hesitated.

One of the initial projects that I contemplated for Waterside Productions was the marketing of a device being created by Andy Kay of Non-Linear Systems called the tutorcomputer. This was a device created for the express purpose of teaching vocabulary using computer technology linked to an audio tape player with words organized, recorded, and defined according to the work of Johnson O'Conner. I had met Andy Kay socially when I was dating his daughter. His daughter and I were mainly tennis partners and friends, but I enjoyed several dinners at Andy's home. We got to talking, and when he told me about his tutorcomputer, I realized that I could help him with a number of aspects of the creation of his program. By chance, the very week I was fired, I had interviewed a young Yale graduate who was interested in working in publishing. Even though I knew I was leaving, I did not cancel the interview scheduled for three P.M. on the Friday that I was to vacate my office. Charles Elster reported for his interview, and was surprised when I told him that I had been fired, and was no longer employed by Harcourt. I talked to him for about forty minutes, and realized that this was a young man who really wanted to be a writer, and was hoping that by working in a publishing company, he would enhance the likelihood of that occurrence. I explained that this was unlikely and that he should just pursue his dream of being a writer, and he should find some suitable employment to support himself while developing his writing skills.

A few months later when Andy Kay revealed his plans for the tutorcomputer and his need for someone to coordinate the recording and editing of the program, I thought of Charlie Elster, the young Yale graduate. I was able to track him down, and in short order, arranged for Non-Linear to hire him. I was indirectly his supervisor, but I was trying to create Waterside and did not take any compensation from Non-Linear for my efforts other than receiving one year exclusive marketing rights to the tutorcomputer. I would go over to Non-Linear once or twice a week to check on Charlie's progress. It was during this time that Andy stumbled upon the creation of the Kaypro computer.

Non-Linear Systems was a progressive company that had created a special type of oscilloscope that was a quantum improvement in the oscilloscope industry. Andy earned a good living from this product, but the company never exceeded ten million dollars in annual sales in its best year. Andy had funded some of the pioneering work of Abraham Maslow and had contributed to many worthwhile projects, including the Johnson O'Conner Foundation. The Foundation had built upon Johnson O'Conner's work, which, coming out of General Electric Corporation in the early 1930s, had postulated that there was a periodic table of human aptitudes. By matching human aptitudes to specific jobs, it was proposed that human beings could perform at maximum efficiency. Along with the human aptitudes, Johnson O'Conner and his colleagues discovered that the most important single correlation with success in business was vocabulary skills. This single indicator was more important than socioeconomic background or educational level in determining success. With this finding in his mind, Andy thought that the most useful contribution he could make was to take the list of words organized in order of importance by the Johnson O'Conner Foundation and create a multimedia learning tool to teach these words to anyone interested in self-improvement. I thought this was a good idea, and a marketable one, and so I contributed my energy. While this was going on, and the company was still supporting itself with the sales of oscilloscopes, another special project evolved into the Kaypro computer. Andy was about a year behind the development of the Osborne computer, but his machine had some enhancements that made it a preferred purchase for many of the first computer users. Overnight, Andy Kay and his Non-Linear Systems was a hundred-million-dollar-a-year business, with expansion and hypergrowth so out of control that he had to bring in circus tents to store computer parts. Luckily, this was Southern California, and it seldom rained.

The computer frenzy was such that there was never any time to devote to the tutorcomputer, and Charlie's project ended up taking years instead of months. I lost out on the marketing opportunity, but benefited from a spontaneous opportunity to start agenting computer books.

On my visits to Charlie, I became friendly with the head of the documentation division. This man was responsible for all of the manuals that accompanied the Kaypro computers. Since software bundling was in vogue in those days, this meant manuals on CPM, dBASE, and Wordstar, as well as the hardware. The head of documentation and his team approached me, and learning of my background in book publishing, asked if I could assist them in getting book contracts to utilize their knowledge on a freelance basis outside of normal work hours as book authors. I checked with Andy, and he saw no conflict with pursuing these opportunities, and overnight I had a dozen qualified computer book writers. This was in early 1983, shortly after the computer had been selected by *Time* magazine as "person of the year." Computer books were hot, and every agent in New York was trying to cash in. Unlike most of the other agents, I at least knew the computer vocabulary. I knew the difference between CPM, dBASE, and Lotus, and this was sacred knowledge back in those days. I was perceived as something of a computer guru, even though I did not own or use a computer myself at the time.

Almost overnight, I sold about fifty titles. I had so much business that I teamed up with a leading New York literary agency, the Barbara Lowenstein Agency, to assist in coordinating the negotiation process. I was earning enough money to cover my basic overhead for the first time since I had started the business in 1982, and I thought that Waterside just might survive after all. It was a pretty heady experience. Barbara and I would go to events like the West Coast Computer Fair, and on the spot sell a twelve book series to Prentice Hall or another publisher, without a scrap of paper other than the list of titles that I would create on the fly, and a list of authors that had some semblance of credentials. This halcyon period lasted for a little over a year, and then the computer book market went totally bust.

Almost every major New York publisher had launched a computer book division simultaneously, and almost every division had chosen to publish the same exact twelve to twenty books. There was a glut of identical titles, and after the initial euphoria, books started to be returned. There were warehouses full of unsold books, and soon just as quickly as these New York publishers had started new divisions, they began to fold them. Some small independents went bankrupt. All in all, it was a bloody scene, and just as quickly as the New York agents had jumped on the bandwagon, they got off. I remember sitting in my office in December of 1983 and thinking that, after five straight months in which more contracts were cancelled than signed, I better go on vacation right away. Either the trend would continue and I would be out of business and unable to take a vacation, or business would pick up again, and I would benefit from getting away from the negative spiral of canceled contracts.

Well, business didn't pick up right away, but it did slow down from the disaster point of view, which was a good thing. I reached a kind of steady state where the number of contracts cancelled and the number of books signed more or less balanced out.

The best part of 1984 for Waterside was that we were able to survive, and the general state of the business was so bad that virtually every single computer book agent, including at the time the mighty John Brockman Agency (which had booked ten million dollars in sales in 1982 alone), withdrew entirely from the computer book agenting business. By default, I was the only agency left standing with any interest or knowledge in computer books. Part of the reason I continued to agent computer books and take calls from authors and computer book publishers was that Waterside had few general interest book authors, so it was either take the calls or do nothing. This was not the case for my more successful competitors, who went back to agenting romance novels, popular science books, or whatever other genres they had been agenting prior to their dalliance with computer books.

I also had a strong sense of ethics, which was a significant contributor to Waterside's success. When a publisher called complaining that they had paid out an advance for a Microsoft Windows book and that they had heard that the product was delayed for another year or two, I was able to convince the author who had received the advance to apply the monies toward a Lotus or WordPerfect book and to deliver a product that could generate some immediate cash flow for both author and publisher. I was also diligent in pursuing claims from authors against bankrupt publishers in quickly getting rights back to unpublished manuscripts, or at least getting advances paid for cancelled books that had been delivered per contract.

One thing led to another, and I started getting referrals not only from my existing authors, but from the few remaining book publishers as well. I was perceived as an honest, ethical, and competent agent who could be helpful in a number of different ways. Several of the editors at the computer book publishing houses were also interested in freelancing as authors themselves, and we started to represent these editors on their own books. This was extremely beneficial for the agency, for when we called an editor, our calls were always answered immediately, since an editor was not sure if we were calling to pitch a book or to report on the progress of pitching their own projects.

By 1985, the agency was once again profitable, and for the first time since founding the company, I was earning almost as much as I had been earning at Harcourt Brace Jovanovich when I had left three years previously. The agency now moved to an actual office overlooking the Del Mar Racetrack. I still only had about four hundred and fifty feet of space, but there was room for a part-time assistant, and there was a great view of the racetrack as well as the beach. Waterside was truly by the side of the water, and I had already achieved my initial goal of being self-sufficient, without the need to return to New York.

My father, with whom I had mended our falling out, was absolutely amazed at Waterside's ability to survive. From his perspective, it defied all the odds. We were in the middle of nowhere, far from the mainstream of book publishing, selling books that until two years ago didn't even exist as a category in most bookstores. It seemed extremely improbable, and I agreed. I kept thinking that the computers were just a fad and that I should cash in now before they disappeared. I did not realize that the industry would continue to grow and that there would be a business that would grow more than forty percent annually for the next twelve years.

In the next chapter, we will explore some of the reasons why the company prospered as consistently as it did and which aspects might be attributed to luck and which to conscious planning. As you will see, very few aspects had to do with conscious planning, but a lot had to do with the ingredients that allow one to create their own luck.

Lessons to Be Learned:

The birth of Waterside

(1) Find a place to make a start and form a goal.

(2) Be flexible about where you start, and be ready to start over if necessary.

(3) Even when down and out, focus on helping others and fulfilling their needs.

(4) Be creative in lowering your overhead. I did this not only with the arrangement with Avant Books, but also in working out my sublease with my attorney friend.

(5) Take risks and invest your time in projects that you think are worthwhile, even if the immediate short-term gain seems unlikely.

(6) Observe what is going on around you and don't be afraid to shift gears. I might never have started agenting computer books if I hadn't paid attention to the computer boom at Kaypro, and I wouldn't have even been aware of what was happening at Kaypro if I had stuck exclusively with my initial focus on making videos and helping a few friends whose books had been cancelled.

(7) Do the right thing. Even when there is chaos and despair around you, focus on doing the right and decent thing. In my case, this meant helping publishers in distress, as well as staying with clients who, through no fault of their own, found their book projects being canceled.

(8) Don't panic. Things looked bleak in 1984, but other than taking a much-needed vacation, I took a wait-and-see approach.

(9) Create a work environment that is nourishing and enjoyable. Give yourself the pleasure of a good view and pleasant surroundings. Surround yourself with relaxed and interesting people. You may make or lose money, but on a daily basis, these small everyday factors of your work environment will have more to do with whether you feel that you are succeeding or failing than the number of sales or canceled contracts.

(10) Take joy in the success of your clients. My greatest joy and sense of purpose came from helping my clients. The pleasure I had when a book was sold and a client was able to realize a dream of becoming a published writer far exceeded any pleasure from calculating what my commission might be on any deal.

(11) When one door closes, another opens. This was true not only when I was sacked at HBJ, opening the door to creating Waterside Productions, Inc., but was also true when the film effort failed, leading to book agenting, and when the tutorcomputer was passed over, leading to the agenting of computer books.

(12) Assume you will be successful from the start and plan for it. The incorporation of Waterside was a symbolic act. I still don't know whether the extra expense of incorporating the way I did was necessary, but psychologically it set the tone for becoming the relatively large and successful agency that Waterside is today.

Key Insight:
AWARENESS

If you can cultivate awareness, you will always be lucky, for you will be aware of the deeper magic of opportunity lurking in the depths of the mundane. It is awareness that turns acceptance of your aptitudes, positive attitude, and willingness to apply yourself into true gold. The deeper your awareness, the richer the ore.

CHAPTER 10

IN THE FLOW: WHY
WATERSIDE PROSPERED

*Daily Miracles and the Creation of a Vortex
of Positive Deal Making Energy. Being
Focused and Loving What You Do.*

The simplest explanation for Waterside's success is that I moved into, and currently maintain, a flow that is entirely supported by the universe. To some extent the flow began with being involved with computers which, in and of themselves, were creating a flow in the larger world economy and transforming life on this planet in the process. Many greater fortunes than mine have been created from this flow, but I had the good sense to feel and see it happening and not resist it.

One of my earliest examples of being in the flow was bumping into someone who knew Alan Simpson. Alan was a psychologist by training, but had become a database specialist by default when he needed to understand computers for his thesis in psychology. When I was starting to agent computer books, I bumped into someone who had just bumped into Alan. Alan had come across Adam Green's *Everyman's Guide to dBASE* and felt that it was so badly written that even he could write a better book. With no more motivation than that, he sat down one Thanksgiving and started writing.

By early spring he had completed the manuscript, but didn't have any idea of what to do with it now that it was written. He just put it on a shelf.

In early March, Alan mentioned to one of his students that he had a finished manuscript and had started to use portions of it to teach his class at UCSD extension. The student bumped into me and related to me a crazy scheme in which he wanted to enlist my help to market solar panels as an energy efficient alternative to traditional heating. I knew nothing about how to market solar panels but mentioned what I was doing (agenting computer books) and an introduction was made.

Alan had been too busy teaching to submit his manuscript to any book publishers. He had been meaning to do some research but just hadn't gotten around to it. I made six copies of the manuscript and sent them out. Within days, an offer came in. It was for $2,000 and Alan was flabbergasted. That seemed like a lot of money to him for something that he had created on a whim and as a personal challenge. He told me to take the offer. I told him that we should wait and see what the other publishers might offer. A second offer came in for $3,000. I called the first publisher back and they upped their offer to $5,000 and offered to make it a two-book offer with the second book to be named later.

Alan was truly amazed. When I told him that I still wasn't ready to accept the offer he started getting nervous. "We don't want to lose this offer. Are you sure you know what you're doing?" He asked. "Yes, I'm sure, don't worry. We can always accept that offer later. It's not going to disappear. Everyone wants a good book on dBASE II." The second publisher eventually came up to $6,000 and also made it a two-book contract. Even better, they did a tremendous job editing the book; it was published and generating royalties within ninety days of accepting their contract offer.

In those days, most computer book publishers paid royalties on a monthly basis. The very first month of publication we received a check for $2,000 indicating that the book had already earned out its $6,000 advance for total royalties of $8,000 in the first month.

I doubted that this had been the case, and warned Alan that we shouldn't cash the check yet because it was likely the publisher had made a mistake. The publisher hadn't made a mistake and we received a check for $8,000 or more, every single month for the next five years from that book alone.

Being in the flow also meant that the job was basically effortless. There were at least a dozen occasions in which a would-be author would walk into my office or call me on the phone, and within minutes, a publisher would call on the other line requesting a title that was ideal for the soon-to-be client I had just met. This happened so many times that I began to be disappointed when it didn't.

One of the reasons that these apparently lucky coincidences would happen was my devotion to doing five or six tasks simultaneously and never refusing to take a phone call. Part of the reason for never refusing to take a phone call had to do with the extremely meager financial resources I had when I started Waterside. I couldn't afford to make a lot of calls and didn't want to have to return calls, so I took every call, even if I was talking to another client or publisher already. I would put whomever I was talking with on hold and promise that I wouldn't be more than a minute. I sometimes had as many as five people on hold simultaneously, but rarely kept anyone waiting more than a minute. I would get right to the point and ask if they were going to make an offer. I knew within a few thousand dollars what every book was worth, and would tell editors what they needed to bid in order to get the book immediately. I would usually ask for three or four thousand dollars more than they wanted to pay. In the beginning, they would balk. After losing books because they had hesitated, they learned that I really did know what their competitors were willing to pay and that I was almost always accurate in telling them what they had to pay to get the book that instant. It soon became apparent that it was worth paying a few thousand dollars more for each book to secure the title rapidly and be able to beat out the competition. In the computer book business even a week lost in trying to find an equivalent manuscript or author would cost the publisher more in lost profits than the slight premium I was asking for my clients. As a result, there was no selling involved in my agenting and no small talk. Editors knew that I had five other people on the line almost continuously and they had to act fast. They knew I would never claim that I could get a price from a competitor unless I really could. I treated all editors and publishers equally and I really did prefer a quick no to a slow maybe, or in some cases, even a slow yes.

It was a different kind of agenting from what most book agents had been used to, and it worked marvelously for me, my clients, and those publishers who rely on Waterside. I attracted the best and the brightest authors and most important, those who were easiest to work with. The industry was moving so fast that just focusing on the major points in each contract—the advance, royalty rates, and the removal of the restrictive option clause was enough. To waste another week quibbling over contract language and other niceties was a disservice to the entire industry. Time would be lost and client and publisher alike would lose opportunities and profits. The industry eventually changed, but for several years my no-nonsense, just-close-the-deal style was vital to maintaining flow.

In those days, flow also meant sheer volume of deals. I personally closed 299 book deals in my most prolific year prior to hiring any other agents. In that year I had one part-time assistant and one trainee assistant. The trainee assistant listened to every negotiation and in two years, without ever having agented a book, was promoted to agent. He was not sure he could handle it, but just as Navajo weavers teach by having their apprentices observe their work and then watch as they finally, without ever having practiced, sit down and weave a perfect cloth, he was flawless. He had typed my letters and listened to every conversation, and when it was time for him to start agenting he had comprehended perfectly my values and unique style of agenting. In fact, I felt he was better than I, because I would observe him handling a negotiation exactly as I would and then he would add his own sense of humor or small twist that was actually an improvement.

When I tried to hire established agents with experience, the process did not work at all, with the higher paid experienced agents selling far fewer books than the neophytes who were asked to file and type letters and then suddenly, after a year or two, were thrust into agenting. It was an interesting process to observe. One young woman came to us fresh from college where she had been a literature major. She was very shy and retiring and I was told by her superior after her first year as an assistant that she was very bright but just didn't have the right personality to be an agent. I felt she deserved a chance anyway. Sure enough, within weeks she was agenting books like crazy and is now up to one hundred titles a year with her own unique personality shining through.

Being in the flow also meant letting employees create their own work schedules. As the company started to grow I needed a full-time secretary/controller. This was very early on, after I had graduated from the dollar-a-page use of the legal secretaries and after my first marvelous part-time assistant who, after threatening to quit every day for the entire two years she worked for me, actually did quit. This woman was extremely bright, extremely talented, and a great typist to boot. She was also a talented writer and artist in her own right. We both knew she was way over qualified for her position and should be doing more with her life. She would come into the office every morning at ten and tell me that she was quitting. I would tell her that I understood but that I would really appreciate it if she would wait until her normal quitting time of one o'clock because we had a dozen contracts to get out that day and I really needed her. She would relent and stay until one, sometimes until two, if there was enough work. When she was ready to leave I would be on the telephone doing a deal, there would be at least one if not two other lines blinking. She would become exasperated and just leave since I didn't have time to coordinate her quitting and severance pay, and since we had become good friends, she couldn't leave without clear closure to our relationship.

This same routine went on for two solid years. Secretly, I think she stayed as much because she pitied what would become of me if she left as well as her own hidden fears about actually taking on the kind of creative work for which she was better suited.

Eventually, she did find a more significant type of work and it was time to hire another employee. I had become spoiled by this remarkable woman who, in three hours a day, was doing the work that most would not have accomplished in eight to ten hours. Partly, she was so productive because she was quick and smart, but I think that a part of her really did plan to quit every day. If you think that it is your last day on the job you can fly through work like nothing because you know you'll never have to do this kind of work again.

I started to interview people and I was particularly taken with a woman who, right up front, told me she had just moved to the area, had a husband who coached the San Diego State football team and four children one of whom was still in elementary school, and that being home at 2:30 when her youngest child was out of school was critical. I thought about it for less than two seconds and told her, "I don't see how that will be a problem. We are starting to get busy here but if you can work from eight until two that should be sufficient. I don't get in until nine myself, but that should give you an extra hour to catch up on the correspondence that I'll create from two to five after you leave." This pattern continued for the entire nine years that this employee worked with Waterside, long after her daughter had graduated from high school and moved away to college. She had become accustomed to her special schedule and it worked fine for me. In the early years I was able to save money by not having to cover a full eight hour work day, and as the company grew and prospered, she was able to receive a salary based on a full day of work, even though she left every day after only six hours.

Another one of my in the flow rules in those early days, was never to go out to lunch. I shouldn't say never, because on those few occasions that a publisher was in town, I might be tempted, but it was rare indeed, less than once a month. I found that not only did I save money by bringing my lunch, but, most important, I saved time. At the height of my one-man-band days I would have trouble even finding the time to eat my brown bag lunch, let alone take time to leave the office. I remember days when I was on the phone nonstop from nine until three or even four, and only then, taking a moment to eat at my desk. For some reason I found this pace more exhilarating than exhausting.

There was no question that I was working hard, but I was working smart. I never went to the office before nine, and once I discovered golf, I would rarely start work before ten. I became a member of the Torrey Pines Six A.M. Brigade with a round of eighteen holes of golf completed every fair-weather working day in San Diego prior to getting to the office. Since it hardly ever rains in San Diego, this meant at least twenty rounds of golf a month for a period of about two years. I went from never having played in my life to breaking 80 and knowing the greens at Torrey Pines like the back of my hand. I also made it a rule to never give out my home phone and to never take a business call at home. I was agenting several hundred books a year and yet kept work hours strictly at nine to five or ten to five with no work on weekends and no work at night. I had young children, and it was an important priority for me to spend evenings and weekends with them, so I never broke this rule in the heyday of Waterside's growth years.

Somehow, despite the imbalance of my crazed working hours, there was balance overall. I couldn't wait to get up every morning, play my golf game (which I constantly was improving), and then get to the office to see what deals could be closed or created that day. This is not to say that all was perfect. There were deals that didn't work out and days in which no deals were made, but these were few and represented but a small minority of the daily successes. I was also immune to rejection from the early days of the agency. Even with successful books, with my abrupt manner I was used to getting four or five no's for every yes. It did not matter; I only needed one yes per book proposal to have a success. Even when a proposal was rejected by everyone to whom it had been submitted, I did not take it as a failure, but a lesson. I would evaluate the reasons for the rejections and encourage the client to either abandon or shelf the project and come up with a better idea that we could sell. On some rare occasions I would resubmit the proposal at a later time to a different group of book publishers.

Perhaps the greatest example for me of being in the flow was my natural tendency to multitask. I was already doing this by having as many as six conversations going on simultaneously, keeping no one on hold for more than a minute. In some cases, I was on the phone the entire day and still needed to do other work so if I only had two or three calls on hold I would also start going through the mail and even typing correspondences. For some crazy reason, while always doing several things at once I seemed to enter an alpha state of pure intuition in which, even if I were only half listening to a client or negotiation, I would come up with dead-on suggestions and rec-ommendations that seemed divinely inspired. It was almost as if I were channeling my advice, with it not really coming from me at all.

I am not sure even today that I really understand my own unique process, but I have been told that by following the disci-plines of meditation and taking time out for breathing, it is possible to create these alpha states of pure energetic impulse. If that is true, then my method must have somehow been the opposite formula for arriving at the same place as the calm and contemplative path. The frenzy and constant activity of my business day created the same kind of calm as the eye of a storm. The storm was all around me but I remained completely detached and calm within. I felt myself almost to be an observer of myself and my negotiations rather than an active participant.

It is hard to describe this vortex of energy that I created. It was not that I did not care about success or failure. I cared on one level very much. I truly felt for my clients, shared the joy of their suc-cesses and the despair of their failures. And yet on another level, I was moving so fast that there was never time to feel any emotion at all. No sooner had a deal been concluded either satisfactorily or been deflatingly rejected than I was on to the next call. Despite my multitasking, that next call was always the most important call, and the one that required, at least in brief intervals, my full and undivided attention.

Lessons to Be Learned:

Being in the flow

(1) Expect miracles every single day.

(2) Consciously multitask whenever possible.

(3) Listen to the human side of people's needs, particularly employees.

(4) Recognize that most people work to live and do not live to work.

(5) Make time for other pursuits beyond work.

(6) Work intensely when you work, but work smarter and not harder, and definitely not longer.

(7) Rejection and failure are part of every business day and are often signals of where to go and what to do next.

(8) Fight like crazy for your goals but detach yourself emotionally from the results of your efforts. The journey really is the reward, and if you forget this you weaken the flow.

(9) Watch and learn from masters. Pattern your actions upon theirs, and then add your own unique touch.

(10) Encourage those who work with and for you, and be willing to take risks with them and encourage them to take risks with themselves.

(11) Be grateful when you are in the flow and appreciate the role of clients and others that make being in the flow possible.

(12) Flowing with the flow and being in the flow are not passive events. Your own energy can harness or impede the flow. Come to every moment with full awareness and the wonder and amazement of a newborn; this will encourage the magic that surrounds you to continue to open you to an even greater magic than you might have at first imagined.

Key Insight:

ABUNDANCE

With true awareness, acceptance, attitude, and aptitude, abundance will follow. Learn that abundance is your birthright. Focus on the joy of life and achievement and the money will follow.

CHAPTER 11

PARTY, PARTY, PARTY

The Role of Trade Shows and
Conferences in Being the Deal

Trade shows and conferences have become essential meeting places at which to conduct business, renew friendships, make new alliances, and introduce new ideas. They serve many purposes and are a great place to let it all hang out and have a good bit of fun in the process. The computer industry took to conferences like ducks to water, with the annual Las Vegas Comdex show and the Consumer Electronics Show being the two not-to-be-missed events with literally hundreds of thousands of attendees filling every hotel, restaurant, and conference exhibit space in all of Las Vegas year after year after year. My participation in these conferences was essential to being in the flow and creating and overseeing deals.

My relationship with the conference mentality started when I was twelve years old and my dad took me to my first American Booksellers Association conference in the basement of the Shoreham hotel in Washington DC. It was Memorial Day weekend of 1962 and it was truly special for me to be invited without my mom to spend the entire weekend with my dad at his most important publishing event. In those days, the ABA consisted of about sixty book publishers, all from New York City, and several thousand independent booksellers. The Memorial Day weekend was chosen because that was the best date for the independent booksellers to take off before the big summer selling season. The trade show was seen as a holiday by everyone as well as an opportunity to examine the forthcoming books for the summer and fall seasons.

In those days, actual books were sold at the show and orders taken. There were special discounts and my father used to write thousands of dollars' worth of business on the show floor every day and in many cases gave extra discounts for cash payments made on the spot. In many instances, these cash payments would end up in the poker pots of the high stakes games played among such luminaries as Bennett Cerf, Nat Wartels, Max Simon, and the other movers and shakers of the New York publishing world.

While these poker games were going on, I would wander around the hotel. Since the entire hotel was filled with publishing executives, it was a pretty safe scene. Almost every publisher had a hospitality suite with an open bar. The fact that I was twelve didn't seem to bother anyone, and in most cases it was just an open bar without any bartender in attendance. I experimented with different beverages and found some that I liked. There were also a number of publishers throwing formal parties and dinners in different meeting rooms. I would wander in, listen to live bands, sometimes find the daughters of other publishing executives in attendance and dance and chat with them.

I worked the booth during the day and met all of Arco's chief customers, so at night I was treated as a legitimate part of the industry and not as merely a child or an intruder. The sales people in particular encouraged me to partake of adult activities, and in many ways, it was at those early ABAs that I continued to attend for the next fifty years that I was truly introduced to the publishing life.

With this kind of introduction to trade shows, Comdex and CES seemed similar, only bigger and better. My operating mode at these events was to start doing business as soon as I reached the airport. In those days, anyone going to the show was a potential author or held some information about a forthcoming product or service that would be worth writing about. Since I had also identified the promotional power of books for computer companies (having created the first official line of company-promoted books for Kaypro and entered initial discussions on the creation of Apple Press, WordPerfect Press, Novell Press and many others), no contact was unconnected at some level with a potential deal.

In many cases, some of my best business deals were done while sharing a cab from McCarron airport to the convention center. Once I arrived at the convention, I would enter through the nearest available entrance and start walking toward any booth that looked inviting. I made a point of visiting all the computer book publishers and the companies whose products we were already writing about. I also had several appointments set up in advance, but in those days, I generated even more business from unplanned meetings and cold calling companies I was not even aware had existed before seeing their booths at Comdex. In many cases, we were able to generate more business from some of the smaller booths manned by just a person or two and offering peanut M&M's to lure potential customers to their booths. One of those small booths turned out to be manned by Pete Peterson of WordPerfect Corporation, which, at the time, was a dwarf compared to WordStar. This led to representing the actual software product itself in a college rights deal that endured even five years later, when WordStar was almost out of business and WordPerfect had taken over, at least for several years, as the dominant word processor in the world.

After a long day of exploring new business opportunities I would hit the party scene. As part of the publishing community, I received Wes Thomas's special insider list of party events. Many were invitation-only events, but Wes was a Waterside client in addition to being a maverick publicist, so we had carte blanche to any event we wanted. In those days it was possible to go up to Bill Gates at a Philippe Kahn toga party and pitch him on doing a book (he turned me down with the excuse that he really wasn't ready for a book then but might be in a few years). It was perceived by the heavy corporate types as extremely cool to be invited to join us at the secret John Dvorak party or some of the more bizarre events such as when Pat McGovern came riding in on a white horse at one of the IDG Magazine celebrations.

Companies went to great lengths to get customer attention with incredible balloons and billboards and parties featuring major celebrities and live acts. The parties were a particularly good opportunity for an agent to pick up new clients, and with such a large base of clients to start with, many of them in attendance, it seemed as though wherever I went I would meet someone who would then introduce me to more potential clients and more potential deals. After a single day, I would have fifty or more plausible leads and after two days I would stop taking business cards because I knew there was no way I could follow up on all the potential business I would create.

I saw my first fax machine at one Comdex and saw a host of new gadgets at each CES show. I had a standard procedure for getting a good location in terms of hotel at every Comdex by rooming with Art Shane, who at the time had a small software company Strawberry Software that provided some measuring tools for the Interface Group that managed Comdex itself. Art had an in and was such a delightful party companion that I never hesitated to pal around with him during the show. He would introduce me to scores of his clients and many of them would either have a need for a book about their products or knew someone else who did.

In the meantime, I continued to attend every ABA as well. These were becoming even more bizarre for me because I was now maintaining at least four if not more realities simultaneously in terms of the friendships and points of reference each group of friends signified for me. Among the older set were people who had known me since I was twelve. To them I was Billy Gladstone, Milt Gladstone's little boy. Then there were the people with whom I had worked at Prentice Hall, Arco, and Harcourt Brace Jovanovich. Each of these groups knew me as a colleague and was interested in how I had fared since going on my own. We had no active business dealings since they were dealing with general books and I with computer books, but there was always a great sense of warmth and familiarity for all of us in reconnecting and being updated on the events of one another's lives. Now there was a new group consisting of the publishers with whom I had been doing business the last several years as a computer book agent. This is where most of the action and most of my focus was. Several strong friendships evolved. Finally, there was the fourth set of acquaintances: people who ran the biggest companies with whom I was making contact related to their interest in moving into electronic media or buying companies that could help them gain a toehold in the computer book segment, which was quickly becoming the most profitable category in all of book publishing.

One year when the ABA was being held in Las Vegas I decided to give a party for all of the computer book publishers and many of my authors. I was celebrating the fact that we had sold our 1250th book and had recently purchased our own building. Just about anyone who was anyone in the industry came to the party and it was an unbelievable success. Part of the reason for the success was that the computer book publishers were extremely distrustful of their competitors and many of the executives at the different companies had never even met each other. There had been an early attempt by Microsoft Press to establish an association of computer book publishers, but Rodnay Zaks of Sybex, among others, was extremely skeptical of sharing any resources or information with Microsoft and the idea died stillborn.

After the party many of the publishing executives called me up to thank me for giving them a chance to meet their contemporaries at other companies, and they suggested that I give a similar party every year. I thought that that might be a good idea until I received the bill for the party. I had spent over twenty thousand dollars, which was not an insignificant sum for a literary agency with only four employees.

I decided that the idea of throwing the party every year was a good one, but that it would be even better if there was a way for the industry to help pay its own way. I hit upon the idea of offering the party the following year as a two-day party to be held in Del Mar near the Waterside office. To make it attractive to book publishers, I decided that there would be speeches during the day to justify the golf, tennis, and special dinners at night. I also decided that I would let my own clients attend for free so that they would have an opportunity to meet personally with the publishers with whom they were doing business. Unlike most conferences, I was more interested in the party than the speeches and was not interested in making money from the conference, but from the commissions that I would earn from the increased deal flow the conference would generate.

I proved to be right in all aspects and soon the Waterside Computer Book and Publishing Conference became the staple of the industry. With feedback from the publishers, we began to invite the heads of the main distribution companies such as Borders and Ingram and to have marketing consultants and industry specialists from Microsoft and other major hardware and software companies in attendance as well. Because we were appealing to a diverse group of authors, publishers, head hunters, venture capitalists, and start-up entrepreneurs, the conference evolved into a stimulating event as well as what became a wonderful three-day party.

The general trade shows as well as our own specific Waterside conference were symbolic of the blurring between fun and deal making. It became my theme that all deals had to be fun as well as profitable and that creating the fun was just as important as creating the deal. In many ways, it became indistinguishable as to where the deal began and the party ended or the party began and the deal ended. This was most particularly true in the case of my relationship with John Kilcullen and the birth of IDG Books and the creation of the For Dummies line (to be described in detail in chapter 13), but let's review the following lessons that effective partying has taught me.

Lessons to Be Learned:
Party, Party, Party

(1) Trade shows and conferences can be great opportunities for dealmakers and deal making if approached with the proper party attitude.

(2) Parties are about having a good time and making friends.

(3) It is never inappropriate to discuss business opportunities at parties focused around business events.

(4) It is easier to do business with friends than with strangers.

(5) It is psychologically comforting to have the continuity of friendships spanning decades that can be formed through annual participation at major industry events.

(6) A good party requires good food, a good location, and interesting, talkative people. Good entertainment can sometimes be helpful, but not if the entertainment interferes with people getting a chance to talk to each other and to know each other better.

(7) At a good party, people who might never have interacted should be brought together to create unexpected connections.

(8) Parties are not the place for serious business confrontations. Only twice has this happened and in both cases it ruined the party for me. I never invited either instigator of the confrontation to a future party or event and still can't understand why in the guise of doing business anyone thinks that that allows them to be publicly rude.

(9) Have a great time but never become so inebriated that you lose your sense of judgment or take foolish risks such as driving while intoxicated. My rule was to never rent a car so that I would never have to worry about endangering myself or others.

(10) Be as wild as you want, but remember that these are all people that you will be seeing again next year and hopefully doing business with for the rest of your life. Act in a way that will not embarrass yourself, your company, or your family.

Key Insight:

APPRECIATION

Once you are in the flow of abundance, the most important single emotion is to show appreciation to yourself and others for your good fortune. Whether you show your appreciation to customers by throwing large parties or just thanking colleagues at work, be sure to appreciate all that you receive and realize that on a deep level your success is due more to the universe than your own will.

CHAPTER 12

THE TRIMTAB FACTOR

How and Where to Focus and the Real
Secrets to Successful Negotiations

I am not a sailor but I attended a wonderful talk by Buckminster Fuller once in which he explained his concept of the trimtab factor. Apparently, there is a small device that controls the direction of a vessel. A small movement of the trimtab makes an enormous difference as to where your vessel will eventually dock.

The principle stuck with me and seems particularly appropriate when discussing deal making and the ability to create your own luck. It is often the minor but significant changes in a contract that determine whether it is a great deal or just a deal. I do not advocate overkill in negotiating contracts. Principally, I believe that the key to all negotiations and all contracts are the people with whom you are negotiating and the integrity they bring to the negotiation table.

Contracts were initially created to put into writing agreements between two equal entities that have goods or services to barter or exchange. The problem from the start, in looking at most contracts today, is that the two parties are seldom equal. This is particularly the case between authors, who are usually single one shop operations, and publishing companies, which are often composed of dozens, if not hundreds, of individuals with millions or tens or even hundreds of millions of dollars at their disposal. This inequality between the two contracting parties, to some extent, gives a lie to the entire process. Strict interpretation of the legal principles upon which contract law was founded could be used as an argument to invalidate any contract between a stronger party and weaker one in which the stronger party takes advantage of its superior strength to muscle unfavorable terms on the weaker party.

I mention this because *real politik* is what governs business today, and it is the balance of power between the two parties that is ultimately more important than any contract language per se. It really is true in many cases that a contract is not worth the paper it is written on if the stronger party chooses to ignore its promises and the weaker party does not have the resources to fight back.

I explain this to my authors and encourage them when they have been taken advantage of by a publisher to avoid working with that publisher in the future and to create extremely successful projects that they can take to the offending party's competitors. Of course, there are always those rare exceptions when taking legal action is appropriate.

In Waterside's own history, we are quite proud that from more than five thousand contracts we have never actually had to go to court to protect ourselves or our clients, and we have had, at most, only one or two legal actions ever taken against us, both of which were relatively trivial and resolved quickly and painlessly without the benefit of legal counsel. I attribute this track record to two things. First, we are very careful in our negotiations to never promise more than we can deliver to either clients or publishers. Second, we have a fair amount of power within our industry and without even making threats can impact future business for publishers that ignore our concerns and those of our clients.

A good case in point concerned the initial contracts for the For Dummies books with IDG. I will explain in greater detail our role in the whole Dummies phenomenon, but the main point here is that the initial contract that we negotiated for our first Dummies authors included a clause that allowed the publisher to cut royalties in half for deep discounting special sales opportunities. Between the time that the contract was negotiated and the time royalties were being paid out, the industry changed dramatically and deep discounts were now everyday discounts. The impact on our collective author pool was considerable, with many millions of dollars in lost revenues at stake.

We explained our position to IDG that although we had a signed contract accepting the special sales provision, the industry changes had made that clause inappropriate and that to enforce it to the letter of the contract was no longer in the spirit of the original agreements. Much to IDG's credit, they understood that to take no action would be unfair to the authors and to Waterside, who they perceived as their partner in initially creating the Dummies line of books. They devised a creative solution that took into account the need for some lessening of author royalties as deep discounting impacted their own margins, but devised a plan that levied this decrease in a gradual way that was tied to the actual discounts being paid rather than to an arbitrary number that had been industry standard at the time the contract was originally created. This small change in language ended up making a difference of many millions of dollars to our clients and also ensured the continuing loyalty of the author base and Waterside upon which IDG's initial success had depended.

Part of my understanding of the trimtab factor is contained in the work smart, not hard principle of Waterside as a company. In negotiations, it is not necessary to make a federal case out of every unfair clause. As a literary agency, we recognize the imbalance of power between publisher and average author. We do not accept gross unfairness, but do accept industry standard inequality. We do not condone out and out unfair play that goes to extremes such as taking author's original ideas and trying to convert them to work-for-hire for a exploiting authors. It is almost as if there is honor among thieves and we expect that minimal level of honor to be upheld. Most important, we do not, deep in our corporate heart, believe that the publisher's unfair advantage in contracts, which they create and which are based on contracts created by other publishers with similar, unfair leverage over authors, is criminal at all.

We would like to see a greater balance of power between authors and publishers, and with the internet and other electronic means of communication becoming ever more pervasive, the balance may be tilting already toward the author side. But as someone brought up on the publishing side of the equation, I am sensitive to the risks that the publishers are taking as well. Being a publisher is not an easy business, and in many cases, without the unfair contracts publishers might not survive at all.

I will never forget a memorable negotiation between my father and his best-selling author, Bernie Gittelson, the creator of the concept of biorhythms. Bernie's first *Biorhythm* book was already on the bestseller list and he walked into my father's office after having treated the entire marketing team and editorial braintrust, as well as my dad, to a wonderful and elaborate luncheon celebrating the number one status of his book. Bernie was a self-promoter and an astute businessman and negotiated his own deals without the benefit of an agent (interestingly, and ironically, given my decision to become a literary agent, Arco had an aversion to book agents and less than one percent of the ten thousand or more books published by Arco were ever purchased from an agent rather than commissioned or negotiated directly with an author). Bernie walked into my dad's office and, in a particularly cheerful tone but still completely serious, asked, "So Milt, do I get the normal screwing on the next contract as well?" My dad just smiled and said, "Of course, why should it be any different?" "Well, I thought I was going to get a little better percentage on the foreign rights and the mass market paperback rights as we had discussed?" Bernie countered. "Oh yes that's true, we're going to give you 75 percent on those rights instead of fifty as I had agreed, but the rest of the contract will be the same. You can think of it as a special screwing just for you rather than the normal screwing," my dad explained as they both laughed.

This was really the trimtab factor at work. Although Bernie had a bestseller and now had some leverage, he was smart enough not to try to change the nature of how Arco did business. He had realized one specific area where Arco was making much more money with little extra effort than it made on the majority of its books for which foreign and mass market paperback rights were not particularly significant and the margins of the effort required relatively standard percentages to be split between author and publisher. In the case of *Biorhythm*, this small change limited exclusively to raising the percent Bernie was to receive on these rights from 50 to 75 percent probably made a difference of tens of thousands of dollars or more on the value of the contract to Bernie. By not trying to make wholesale changes in the contract he had negotiated with my dad, a man with whom it was almost impossible to negotiate with at all, Bernie gained a significant concession. At the same time, Bernie recognized the basic unfairness of the author–publisher contract and did not make a big deal out of it. There was trust and mutual respect between the two men, and they knew that each would be rewarded fairly (at least by industry standards) for their contributions to the next bestseller Bernie would write.

I encourage this focus in all contract negotiations. Focus first on the people and then on the one, two, or three truly significant points in the contract. In some cases, minor modifications to these significant points are achievable and will make a much greater difference in where your financial vessel will eventually dock than making major changes in the hundred or more clauses that are not essential and that in the end have little or no impact on your final financial situation unless there is that one-in-a-thousand occurrence of a book selling a hundred times more copies than anticipated, a company going bankrupt, or some other odd occurrence for which it is almost impossible to plan.

Of course, once you are a household name and you can predict that your books or products will generate tens or hundreds of millions of dollars in revenues, then many of these small and trivial possibilities need to be given thorough review and outside lawyers or experts need to be consulted. But these are the exceptions and not the rule and, usually in these cases, special forms of contracts have evolved over time for special situations and special clients so that even then, each contract really only requires concentration on the main points.

This ability to know how and when to focus is the most important skill for a negotiator to have. I have been told by industry executives that before negotiating a deal directly with me they had heard that I was a ruthless and hard negotiator. I was amazed that anyone who had actually negotiated with me could feel this way, but I didn't doubt the veracity of these reports and tried to fathom how they came about. I suppose that my absolute confidence during a negotiation that I was probably right about price and therefore relatively inflexible might be seen as ruthless to someone who did not really understand the business or what they were doing. From my perspective, I was being efficient and honest and cutting to the chase. A negotiation should be about coming to terms and deciding on a course of action, not about making friends. There might be time to make friends later and it might be a good idea for the two parties that eventually sign the contract to become friendly, but as far the negotiator's or agent's role is concerned, that is not important at all. For long-term relationships, it helps, and I have found myself doing deals with the same people over and over again. Once someone accepted and understood the boundaries of any negotiation with me, I truly believe that they found me a soft rather than hard adversary and a relative pleasure to negotiate with because I knew what was important to me and didn't waste a lot of time with secondary issues.

As the computer book industry evolved, it came to pass that Waterside represented about twenty-five percent of the entire market. Que, later purchased by Macmillan and then merged with Sams Publishing, came to represent twenty-five percent as well; however, there was no communication or business done between the two companies.

This had evolved due to a misunderstanding between the original founder of Que publishing, Dick Summi, and myself. In the early days of the industry, when Que was just an idea in Dick's mind and before he had executed getting the right books to market quickly, he was a relatively unknown publisher struggling from the unlikely location of Indianapolis. At the time, Waterside was a relatively obscure agency from Del Mar, California, struggling to survive. I ended up meeting Richard Swadley on his first business trip as the new assistant to editor Bill Oliphant of Howard Sams Publishing. He had gone to one of the early West Coast Computer book fairs when it was still held in Brooks Hall and was a hotbed for roller skating promoters and other outlandish stunts. Richard and I met regarding a project, which Waterside was representing, and eventually signed with his boss.

A few months later, Richard called me and told me that he had some ideas for his own books that didn't really fit in with the publishing program at Sams, and he had permission to write them on his own time for another publisher if he could find one. He asked me if I could help, and I signed Richard up as a client and submitted his proposal for a series of books. I sent the proposal out as a multiple submission and included the newly started Que in the list. Well, Dick Summi looked at the address for the author on the proposal and saw that he was from Indianapolis where Dick and Que were located. Dick didn't understand the need for an agent and thought he could save time and money by contacting Richard directly. This is something that the ethic of established book publishing would never condone, but Dick wasn't coming from the established book-publishing norm. He was a straightforward entrepreneur who had stumbled into book publishing without any real training in its mores and ethics. Richard had the good sense to call me when Dick showed up on his doorstep and offered him $1,000 to sign and tried to hard pressure him into signing on the spot, without conferring with me. I had already secured a seven thousand dollar advance for the same book from Prentice Hall, which was an established and reputable company, and so informed Dick Summi that he would have to improve his offer if he hoped to sign Richard. Dick chose not to respond directly to me at all but decided from that day forth he would insist that every author who signed a Que contract would have to agree not to be represented by an agent. I thought this was a bit of an overreaction given that he had tried to screw me, not me him, but that was his reaction. We had different worldviews and he didn't think he needed me and I knew I did not need him.

We both prospered, and a few years later Dick sold the company to Macmillan and left the business for his next entrepreneurial pursuit which, at that time, had something to do with helicopters. Before Dick left the company he had hired a bright young attorney who also was an accredited accountant. This attorney started out handling contractual matters and later foreign rights, and he eventually was made president of the company when Dick left. His name was Scott Flanders.

At the time, Que had a terrible reputation with book authors. They were notorious for taking advantage of authors, insisting on work-for-hire agreements, paying minimal or no royalties, and generally treating authors as a frangible commodity with little perceived value. The joke in the industry was that Que was looking for a way to have computers write their books so that they wouldn't have to deal with authors at all.

It turned out that both Mr. Flanders and I decided to attend one of Stewart Alsop's early Agenda conferences back in the days when they were held at La Costa Resort, right outside of San Diego. The agenda of the conferences back then were extremely relevant for the computer book publishing business. The wars between Microsoft, Lotus, Ashton-Tate, and Borland were still being fought, and you could gain some insight as to who had the upper hand and who was likely to prevail, and therefore which products would be the best to have authors writing about and books being written about. Scott and I ended up sitting together at one of the sessions, and when we met, we were surprised by how much we had in common. Scott explained that many of the initial book series had been created in house and that they saw no need to pay royalties on concepts that they had more-or-less invented themselves. I appreciated that perspective and told him how similar it was to the philosophy that had contributed to my Dad's company Arco, which, since it had invented the test prep line of books, also shunned from paying royalties to authors in most cases as well. At the same time, I explained to Scott that in those cases where the ideas were coming from the authors and when the execution by an individual author was superior, it made sense to reward such creativity with full author status and industry standard royalties. He saw my point and suggested that we play a round a golf. The round of golf led to many rounds of golf and many dinners together, and we ended up being good friends with mutual respect for the way we were running our businesses. Scott eventually decided to drop the company-mandated prohibition against working with authors who had agents, and over time, Waterside and Que and its growing list of imprints were doing business together.

Instead of trying to change each other's worldview and business model, Scott and I focused on areas where it made sense to work together. The flexibilities were not great for either party, but starting with the initial small yet significant removal of the prohibition against working with agents, we made a few inroads relating to royalty structures from his end and work for hire exceptions on ours. We did not thrash through the many still unfair clauses in many of the Que contracts, but we focused on a few major issues that justified working together and focused on opportunities that in the long run would add to the profitability of Que, while also producing fair fees for our authors.

Learning to focus and knowing what to focus on is a lifelong challenge. To some extent, the first step is to be steeped in an industry and to intimately understand the basic principles that generate workflow, sales, and profits in your domain. I grew up in a book publishing family and learned this almost by osmosis, so that for me, it has almost always been a primarily intuitive experience, at least in book publishing and book agenting. As I step into new areas such as mergers and acquisitions and venture capital fundings, it takes me longer before I am certain that I am focusing on the true fundamentals in any decision or negotiation. One of the ways that I have helped accelerate my own growth is to find people in their fields who are as successful in what they are doing as I have been in publishing. I learn from these people and start to mirror them. If I choose the right people, I learn very quickly what they focus on in these new arenas or even new industries and become a master along with them.

One of the venture-level dealmakers and investors who I have learned from is Ron Posner. Ron has been written up as the Mr. Goodwrench of Silicon Gulch in San Francisco for his ability to help small firms merge with larger entities to achieve critical mass and economies of scale. Like any player, Ron has his critics as well as his fans and has had his share of failures as well as successes. Personally, I have found Ron to be a no-nonsense and straightforward negotiator and businessperson who gets directly to the meat of every negotiation. Ron has demonstrated a particular skill in getting in and getting out of deals profitability and he has contributed some insights to this book in chapter 14, which are compatible with my own philosophy of being the deal. Perhaps most important for me, Ron is a relaxed individual who enjoys life and appreciates the environment of the deal-making process as much as the deal itself.

I first met Ron when he was the CEO for Peter Norton Computing. Ron was hired specifically to position the company for a public offering or a sale to a larger entity. Peter had taken the company as far as he was comfortable and had the good sense that many entrepreneurs lack to know when it was time to exit. Fortunately for Peter, he also had many significant interests outside of work to help him with the transition.

Ron did a marvelous job of both positioning the company and negotiating its sale to Symantec. I had had very little direct contract with Ron as Peter's literary agent, since in general Peter's books were kept separate from the company itself. There was one line of products that crossed over that I had been asked to save a rather large negotiation and in which I performed as required. The fee for this work was relatively large, since I did everything on a commission basis and the deal itself was worth over a half-a-million dollars. The company attorney had ended up playing a significant role in the final negotiation and had wanted my normal commission reduced by an amount to be negotiated in good faith. I was not particularly open to a major reduction, but under the circumstances did allow that it was a special case and that I was willing to negotiate. The negotiations had dragged on for several months and suddenly the company was to be sold without my commission having been paid.

I called up and expressed my concern, and I demanded a payment of the full commission immediately. It took a few days and instead of receiving a call back from the attorney, I received a call directly from Ron. "Bill, I have a real problem. I know that you are entitled to your commission, but the way I negotiated the deal with Symantec, Peter is receiving a multiple based on revenues and earnings. If we pay you your full fee it will cost Peter over a million dollars of his share of the proceeds from the sale. This slipped through the cracks and wasn't brought to my attention until we had already given final financials to Symantec. I do have a small miscellaneous emergency category and I can send you a check for ten thousand dollars today and owe you a big favor in the future if you can accept that."

Ten thousand dollars represented but a small fraction of the total commission to which I was entitled but I did not hesitate. I accepted Ron's proposal reminding him, "All right, but you owe me really big time and I am taking you at your word that you won't forget." "You can count on it. Thanks a lot. Both Peter and I really appreciate you doing this."

In my mind, it was a no-brainer to accept a significantly reduced commission. First of all, there was no way I was going to take action against a company owned by one of my best clients. Second, I had no reason to doubt the veracity of what Ron was telling me. I knew that in general terms what he was saying made sense about the way Peter's price was probably calculated, having observed similar formulas in past publishing mergers such as Arco from firsthand experience. There was also something completely disarming about Ron's candor and outrageous proposition. I might have been able to argue and double the amount that he was offering me, but to what end? I would still be accepting a small fraction of the entire fee and I would not receive enough additional money to make a significant difference in my personal financial fortunes for that year. I let it go and never regretted that decision, even though I have yet to collect in any direct way on that favor, other than by forming a social friendship with Ron that has included some delightful days of skiing in Aspen and hiking in Kauai.

Lessons to Be Learned:

Trimtab, focused negotiating:

(1) Do not negotiate a contract until you are familiar with the terrain.

(2) Once familiar, focus on the main points only.

(3) Determine up front the other side's flexibility, if any, on main points.

(4) Focus on what the other side is hoping to achieve and learn as much as possible about their business culture and their goals.

(5) Be inflexible on your own key points.

(6) Be flexible and even willing to break your own rules under extraordinary circumstances or with extraordinary people.

(7) Always take the long view in all business relationships.

(8) Recognize the basic inequalities, if any, in each negotiation before becoming involved.

(9) Recognize that the people behind the contract are more important than the words in the contract.

(10) Do your homework and be sure that you share a similar worldview or business view with your opposition. If you don't, there can be misunderstandings and you are likely to be taken advantage of. If you can develop mutual respect and trust with your adversary, you are less likely to be taken advantage of later.

CHAPTER 13

I'M A DUMMY; THEY'RE ALL DUMMIES; WOULDN'T YOU LIKE TO BE A DUMMY, TOO (AUTHOR THAT IS)?

The Creation of IDG Books and the For Dummies Phenomenon: A Case Study of Setbacks Leading to "Instant Success"

IDG Books Worldwide and their creation of the line of For Dummies books is truly a publishing phenomenon. There has never been a book series in the history of publishing that generated so many titles and so many sales so quickly. More than two-hundred million-plus copies of For Dummies books have been sold; IDG Books went public and was later sold to John Wiley Publishing for more than eighty million dollars. The company was funded with less than ten million dollars. Everyone involved, including present owner Wiley, Has benefited significantly from the For Dummies book series.

In April 1997, IDG published its own version of the "Dummies Success" Story. It is mostly accurate, presents the basic facts well, and is reproduced with permission from IDG.

The IDG Books Worldwide, INC. "DUMMIES" Success Story
How the "little book publisher that could" became the fastest growing publisher in the country

In 1987, over dinner with a friend, John Kilcullen was kicking around some new ideas for computer books. Kilcullen, who at the time worked for Bantam Doubleday Dell Publishing Group in New York, was recalling a remark made by a customer in a Software Etc. store who requested a book on the DOS operating system. He said, John remembered, that he needed a simple, basic book because he didn't know anything about computers. "Something," the customer suggested, "like DOS for Dummies."

The idea was filed away in Kilcullen's head until he was in California four years later as the cofounder and Publisher of IDG Books Worldwide in San Mateo, California. Attending a publishers conference, Kilcullen heard author Dan Gookin speak. With humor and irreverence, Gookin criticized the publishing industry's lack of creativity and accused them of tearing apart his manuscripts and turning them into formulaic, cookie-cutter books. It was at that moment that Kilcullen discovered the author of the bestselling computer book of the '90's-IDG Books Worldwide's *DOS For Dummies*®.

The idea was very simple: identify with the anxiety and frustration people felt about technology by poking fun at it with books that are insightful, educational, and made learning easy and interesting. Add a strong dose of personality with entertaining cartoons providing comic relief and you've got ... *For Dummies*®. Patrick McGovern, Founder and Chairman of International Data Group (IDG), the world's leading source of information on information technology, supported Kilcullen in his conviction to publish the unconventionally titled book when many industry pundits turned their noses at the idea. In November 1991, 7,500 copies of *DOS for Dummies* rolled off the press six months after the release of MS-DOS version 5.0— certainly not "day and date" as is the hallmark of computer book bestsellers.

DOS for Dummies was initially met with a lot of skepticism. In fact, the largest bookstore chain in the US refused to buy *DOS for Dummies*. First, critics said the book was too late—that reference books must be released almost simultaneously with the hardware or software product in order for them to sell well. IDG Books Worldwide was also accused of insulting the reader with its... *For Dummies®* branding strategy. Kilcullen responded by calling the title a "term of endearment" that readers could immediately relate to and identify with. But it wasn't just the smart branding strategy that made the book so successful; Kilcullen built a marketing machine that touched millions of readers around the world.

After reading an article in *Forbes* about the psychological values people associate with certain colors, Kilcullen changed the original cover to bright yellow and black in order to attract attention and draw the reader to pick it up. The sell was easy after that. Marketed as a "reference book for the rest of us," the text came alive through the animation of IDG Books' Dummy character and the icons that guided readers to key points throughout the book. Chapters were neatly divided into sections that made logical sense so that the reader could immediately find information that was needed and skip over the "technical stuff." The text, lightly simmered in humor, was designed to be informative yet entertaining. In fact, hundreds of readers have commented on how the... *For Dummies®* titles are the only computer books that make them laugh out loud.

Less than six years after the publication of *DOS for Dummies*, IDG Books Worldwide celebrated the publishing of 30 million... *For Dummies* books. Kilcullen leveraged IDG Books' international distribution network and currently has... *For Dummies®* titles in 32 foreign translations, many of them the # 1 bestsellers in their local markets.

Kilcullen attributes IDG Books' phenomenal success to the company's philosophy of staying close to the customer and alleviating the frustration they feel toward confusing subjects, such as technology. In April 1994, IDG Books ventured outside of the technology topics and published *Personal Finance for Dummies*™ by Eric Tyson.

Within three weeks of its publication, the book sold out in bookstores across the United States. Recently, IDG Books Worldwide released *Personal Finance for Dummies*, 2nd Edition, which continues to dominate business bestseller lists across the country. IDG Books Worldwide has also published other general interest titles for its ... *For Dummies*® readers, including *Sex for Dummies*™, *Gardening for Dummies*™, *Fitness for Dummies*™, *Cooking for Dummies*™, *Investing for Dummies*™, *Red Wine for Dummies*™, and *White Wine for Dummies*™.

Beyond the sales figures, Kilcullen recognizes that at the core of IDG Books' success is the common belief throughout the organization that anything is possible. The Chairman of IDG invested in Kilcullen when no one else would, the authors wrote for IDG when it was merely a twinkle in the founder's eye, and the employees kept a high level of energy and strong work ethic regardless of what the critics had to say about their products. The organization as a whole holds a common vision of making readers wealthy with knowledge, which in turn makes the publisher, the author, and the reader happy. The passion to help people understand confusing topics has driven IDG Books worldwide from a start-up to an industry leader and has propelled the organization from the "little book publisher that could" to the fastest growing publisher of computer and general reference books in the country.

As I said, all of what is reported above is correct, but as John Kilcullen likes to say, "Success has many fathers," and my version as well as Dan Gookin's version of the story would be somewhat different. I consider John a good friend and IDG a wonderful company to partner with, so rather than quibble, let me just present the rest of the story, parts of which are even unknown to John.

The real start of the IDG phenomenon began in 1986. Waterside was just beginning to pull out of the disaster of 1984 when the bookstores had shipped back every identical first book of computing except the Peter McWilliams book, which had sold several hundred thousand copies. Except for that title, every bookstore buyer with a memory vowed that they would never again sell a low-level computer book. They had been killed by trying to sell that type of book and had learned their lesson. Give people intermediate and advanced books with real meat for the serious computer user and leave introductory books alone.

This philosophy persisted for years. Starting in 1986 and at least once if not twice a year thereafter for the next five years, I would receive from my authors proposals with titles like *Computing 101, Computing for Idiots, Computing for Simpletons, Computing for the Technologically Handicapped, Computing for the Technophobic, Computing for the Technical Illiterate,* etc. Some of these proposals were by name-brand authors with well-thought-out tables of contents and good ideas. Every single time I would send these proposals out to half a dozen or more of the established computer book publishers and every time they would come back with comments like, "I really like it and got it through the publishing committee, but when we checked with the buyer at Walden we were told that he wouldn't touch it with a ten foot pole—sorry" or "Well executed but the book buyers will never go for it." Either way, it spelled rejection, and I would console the author, telling him to go write another book on Lotus or something that we could sell more easily.

At the same time this was going on, as part of Waterside's corporate strategy I was pursuing the representation of individual companies and magazines. Of all the magazines, my favorite was *Infoworld. Infoworld* was an IDG publication specializing in information about computers, computer software, and other topics of specific interest to MIS managers and anyone who was thinking of computerizing their business. I discovered the publication at one of the early Comdexes and started to subscribe right away. It was the only industry magazine to which I subscribed because I did not have time to read a lot and this single magazine through the 1980s told me everything I needed to know. I was not particularly sophisticated about computing and generally I just used to look at the ads. By looking at the ads, I could tell which hardware and software companies were releasing new products and how large their marketing and ad budgets would be. Whenever I saw a new product with a full-page ad, I would immediately track down the company, find out a few additional details, and start calling Waterside authors with the suggestion that they check out the new product and if they liked it, to write a book proposal. This was extremely effective for learning about the industry and new trends with relatively little effort.

In the course of becoming so fond of *Infoworld* magazine, I also became friendly with several of their editors and freelance contributors ranging from Stewart Alsop to John Barry to Michael McCarthy. I would pester these editors about writing books since they had some recognition in the industry through their columns in *Infoworld,* but in most cases, they were just too busy. Never one to give up easily, I decided to approach the proposition in a different way altogether and set up a meeting with Jonathan Saks, then the managing director of *Infoworld.* I suggested that Jonathan allow Waterside to package a series of *Infoworld* books and that Waterside would help out if necessary by providing additional writers if *Infoworld* columnists were too busy. I suggested that the book would be good PR for the magazine and could also be a significant revenue stream to be shared between *Infoworld* and the authors.

Jonathan agreed and Waterside did its part arranging for a publishing relationship and helping to launch a modest but successful line of books. About two years later in 1989 I received an unusual call from Jonathon, "Bill, I'm tired of running *Infoworld* and told Pat McGovern that I was quitting but he wouldn't let me. He told me that I could leave *Infoworld* if I really wanted to, but that he was willing to back me in any other logical venture that I might choose. I told him that I would think about it and what I'm thinking about is creating a book publishing company to publish technical books. Is this is a crazy idea or not? I've done a little research and there seems to be plenty of technical publishing companies out there, but I am still intrigued by the idea. What do you think?"

"You are definitely crazy. There are too many computer book publishers out there already, and some of them are starting to have tough times again. But for IDG I think this makes a lot of sense.

You can use IDG publications to promote the books and other IDG organizations to help determine which books to publish and even as a potential source of authors. As far as Waterside is concerned, we are beginning to get uncomfortable with the growing market dominance of Que/Macmillan and anything we can do to help, we will. We would love to see another strong, author-oriented book publisher out there, and you know how much I admire what you and your staff have done at *Infoworld*," was my response.

"I haven't made up my mind, but if I do this, Mac has already agreed to come aboard as editor. We'll both be attending the Software Publisher's conference at the Hotel Del Coronado next week. Why don't you join us for lunch?"

The next week, I had two lunches. The first was with Jonathan Saks at which he told me he had decided to go forward. He asked me to help him with a list of names of top marketing people who might be available to help him with his start up. One of those names was John Kilcullen, who I knew only casually from visits to Bantam where I had heard good things about him. I also gave Jonathan leads as to which distributors to talk to and other general information that a start-up would find useful. The second lunch was with Mac. At that lunch, even though there was no such entity as IDG books, we negotiated a contract for Waterside client John Goodman for a book about an esoteric software product named *The Official Spinrite Companion*. The advance was $5,000 and I was told that corporate policy was that $5,000 would be the top advance for all books in the first year. I explained that this would make it difficult to sign up top Waterside clients but that we would still help as much as we could. I suggested that if they could just go to ten or twelve thousand dollars, they would start to be competitive with Bantam and others and would have a much better chance of getting A-list authors.

IDG books had a very rough first year. They got involved with doing some full color game strategy guides with their sister company GamePro that lost a lot of money and their initial books were midlist titles that were not gathering the kind of distribution that was necessary for truly profitable book publishing. Eventually, Jonathan Saks decided that he wanted to do something else and John Kilcullen was elevated to the head spot.

By now, it was spring of 1991 and I was still sending out my annual low-level introduction to computers book proposal and getting it rejected because the retail book chains wouldn't take any copies. One of those proposals went to Mac, editor-in-chief of IDG. I don't know if John ever saw that proposal, but a few weeks later, we held the first annual Waterside author and publishing conference (the conference mentioned in IDG's official version of the Dummies story). Dan Gookin was one of the speakers and he did go into his cookie-cutter story and subsequently Mac, John, and Dan got together and came up with a modification on Dan's recently submitted book proposal that became the Dummies book. I don't question that John was thinking along these same lines on his own, because when the offer first came in it was presented as work for hire based on IDG's idea. I explained that except for the title, the idea was pretty much what Dan had been proposing and that by using a quality author like Dan instead of the kind of beginning author that might agree to a work for hire contract they would get a much better book. My argument must have been convincing because in the end, the contract called for royalties instead of a flat fee. This single adjustment in that contract ended up generating tens of millions of dollars in royalties over the years, to Dan and other authors and also ensured the consistent high quality of the Dummies books being able to attract name brand and highly talented authors rather than degenerating into tired formula writing.

I have no doubt but that the official story of the "largest bookstore chain in the US refused to buy *DOS for Dummies*" is entirely correct. It was this same chain that year after year convinced the rest of the industry to pass on titles similar in scope and approach to *DOS for Dummies*. Had IDG been in the business longer they probably would have felt doomed from the start and not signed the book. Because they were new and were less connected than other publishers, they were not astute enough to determine that the major chain would pass on the title before entering the Gookin contract. They probably felt erroneously that they could turn that buyer around once they had a published book. All the other publishers knew it wouldn't work and stayed away.

To some extent, I would say that the decision to publish the first Dummies book was a case of dumb luck, but on another level, it was pure brilliance. Despite the odds, the entire company focused on what they knew was a really great idea and, as a team working closely with Dan Gookin, added their own creative input and created a truly great book, humorous, fun, easy to use, and extremely useful to the average book buyer. They stuck with their convictions and, despite the initial rejection of the bookstore distribution system, didn't give up on the book. Once they broke through the distribution logjam, the result of hyper-success was almost predictable. I had been telling everyone for years that my authors were being told by their students that there was a demand for these low-level books, but having been burnt before, the bookstores and major computer book publishers were unwilling to be burned again with low-level books. This created a vacuum on the low-level side of the market in that no low-level books were published between 1984 and the 1991 release of *DOS for Dummies*. When the book hit in mid-1992, it created a groundswell that altered the landscape of the entire computer book publishing industry. Other companies tried to play catch-up, introducing DOS for Idiots and similar titles, but through excellent execution and clear vision in signing up the best possible authors to continue the Dummies series. as well as Dan Gookin's own hyperproductivity at the time, IDG Books won the day and expanded upon the series in text book fashion, bringing to book publishing the power of branding as it had been traditionally applied to other industries.

Throughout this whole success story, John Kilcullen and I developed a significant friendship. The basis for this friendship was not only the business we were able to generate together but the fun we had doing it. Both John and I enjoy good food and wine and champagne. We were particularly fond of Spanish tapas and gourmet starters or appetizers. We would start all of our meetings with a lunch, dinner, or in between snack. Some of these meetings were in San Francisco, some in San Diego, some in airports; it hardly mattered where. Our task was to find the best possible place whatever the hour and order the best food and champagne we could find. Only after this important part of our meeting was taken care of did we plot the next titles and authors to expand the Dummies series. Some major best-selling books came from these food and wine fests, but more time was devoted to the menu than the negotiations. It was always such a treat when John and I got together that new ideas for books would emerge that neither of us had contemplated when we first scheduled the meetings. It got to the point that we would schedule meetings whether or not we had a specific agenda, just for the fun of it with oftentimes unexpected, yet from a business perspective, significant titles either signed or issues resolved.

One of the best aspects about John was his set of wide-ranging interests, from sports to the arts to fashion. John was focused on his business and was an incredible salesman for his concepts, but he was not limited to his immediate goals. He had a wider view of both business and of life, and in sharing his wider interests made himself a more appealing colleague with whom to interact. In the end, this led to an extremely close relationship between Waterside and IDG books that, particularly in the early years of IDG, was essential for their survival and growth.

Lessons to Be Learned:
The Success of Dummies
   (1) An "instant success" can sometime take many years.
   (2) Industry experts are not always correct.
   (3) It can sometimes be an advantage to start late, because in starting late, you are starting fresh.
   (4) Once you make a commitment to an idea, put everything you have behind it and don't allow initial resistance to defeat you.

(5) Once you have initial success, keep your focus and expand on it.

(6) Stay close to your customers, your suppliers, your authors, and your employees.

(7) Do not be afraid to experiment. Most computer book publishers would not have ventured into the areas of finance, cooking, sex, and wine.

(8) Learn from the past but don't fall victim to ignoring changing times.

(9) Make learning fun and humorous.

(10) Focus as much on the fun of your success as on the success itself.

CHAPTER 14

GETTING IN AND GETTING OUT

A Primer on Maximizing Gains in the Shortest Possible Time Frame by Steering Luck, Timing, and Opportunity in Your Direction

*A*s mentioned previously, Ron Posner is a friend and colleague. Ron has a unique sense of humor and a wonderful track record of business success. Ron is more cynical than I, but his advice resonates. Ron's insights in his own words:

1. Overall philosophy

The most important lesson I've learned over the course of many deals is the need to carefully structure your own stock deal with the company on the way into the company (salary doesn't matter) or start-up, and how to control and structure your exit package on the way out to maximize capital gains for you and for the rest of the shareholders; everything in the middle is called "work."

When I was speaking to a group of undergraduates a while back, I was part of a panel on career planning with representatives from IBM and AT&T. After the audience heard about working your way up to VP in twenty-five years, I was introduced as the entrepreneur in the group that may have another point of view—and yes, I did. Basically, I told the assembled crowd that there is no such thing as career planning and that you just need to keep your eyes open for opportunities and be smart enough to recognize them when they came sailing by.

There are some in the high-tech industry who say I don't stick with companies long enough and sell them too early. To those folks I say, "Show me the money." Since the technology changes every two years or so, fifty percent and one hundred percent every four years, it's very difficult to stay ahead of the curve without large resources of Microsoft, Compaq, Cisco, etc., so the need to consolidate is great. As a result, I start planning to sell the company the day I arrive, if not the day before. You can't stand still in the high-tech environment, or maybe any business environment, these days. As they say, the only constant is change, and as I say, "Merge, purge, or get out of the way."

2. Deal Stories:

I learned some of my first lessons in deal making at the foot of the masters: Art Rock, Sandy Kapan, and Max Palevsky sold Scientific Data Systems to Xerox for $1 billion, or 10-times sales, in the late '60s. SDS and DEC at that time were two of the highest-flying high-tech companies around, and I was just hired out of Harvard business school to go to work at SDS (at the time, DEC didn't believe in paying its salesmen a commission, and the weather was much better in Santa Monica where SDS was based than in Boston where DEC was). SDS had just reached a $100 million in sales in selling computers for scientific, government, and educational purposes, when Xerox came shopping because they just had to have the computer company under their wings. (Lesson #1: There's nothing better in deal making than to find a large, hungry buyer who isn't going to be provided enough time to perform proper due diligence). Xerox paid this unheard of price then (even now) and tried to turn the company into a business data processing company, losing many of the hard-driving salespeople who made the company successful in the first place. Three years later, it was hard to find what was left of the company. Located in his retirement villa in St. Jean Cap Ferrat, France, Paul Putney, the VP of Personnel at SDS at this time and after the merger one of the executives who moved back to Xerox headquarters in a senior role, said, "You couldn't have found a more hungry buyer who did less due diligence in a shorter period of time than Xerox." Needless to say, all of the executives made millions on their stock options (and that was a point in time when a million dollars meant something). Shortly after this sale, the VP of Sales, the head of sales training, and I left to start a training company, called Tratec, that we eventually took public and sold to McGraw Hill.

a. The Ghost of George Tate and L. Ron Hubbard Meets the Samurai CEO ... the Ashton-Tate Deal.

After starting another training company called NTS and selling it to Safeguard Business Systems, part of the Safeguard Scientific Group Company, I decided to join an industry just starting to take off: the PC software industry. I looked around for a company in my own backyard of LA, and found through my then six-year-old daughter, who was jumping rope with the daughter of the newly installed president of Ashton-Tate, then just starting to take off. The girls were singing, "Five, six, pick up sticks, seven, eight, Ashton-Tate," which caused me to ask my daughter's girlfriend how she knew about Ashton-Tate, and her response was, "My daddy works there and we just moved up the street." So following my own advice of seeing an opportunity go by my nose, I asked the little girl to bring her dad down to have some wine on my balcony in Malibu.

When I joined Ashton-Tate full-time, it was to find a chaotic work environment, which was true of the whole industry. No one had any job-related experience for the positions they were holding. For example, the woman running production was using the Scientology manual to make most of her production decisions. After George Tate died at a young age in his office, things started to get weird there, including one of the board members asking to check with George on an important decision, who he claimed visited him regularly at night to discuss company policy, and the CEO who came to work with a tie wrapped around his head and asked for us to call him the samurai CEO from then on.

The beginning of the end came when the board decided to bring professional management into the company: It works fifty percent of the time. In this case, the new CEO felt all executives were plug replaceable, like the software, and the company was later sold for a fraction of its true value. However, in the meantime we took the company public and got the stock to go from five to fifty by being in the right place at the right time as the PC software industry was taking off around us. By the time I left three years later, we had grown the company from $10 million when I arrived to over $200 million in sales. Another lesson in luck, timing, and recognizing opportunity on the jump rope sidewalk.

Ron intended to add more stories to this chapter, but never did. His list follows and we can only imagine the details. Even without the details, we can garner some "Lessons to be Learned."

(Outline for the rest of the chapter)
b. "You're Fired...Now Sell Me Your Company"...The Peter Norton Computing Deal with Symantec
c. The French Connection: The Ansa/Borland Deal
d. The Catfood Boys: The WordStar/Spinnaker/Softkey Deal (Seymour: I Could Have Been Bill Gates").
e. Never Underestimate the Value of Having an Existing Market: The GZ Deal

Lessons to Be Learned:
The best time to sell your company is when someone asks to buy it.
Stock options pay off, so don't worry about your salary.
How to make luck and timing work in your favor.
And best of all: get someone else to do all of the hard work (Peter Norton).

Chapter 15

Putting It All Together

The Seven-Step Program for Creating Your Own Good Luck in Business. The Seven As and the Three Ps

The stories you have read in this book are all true; some of them are amusing, some informative, and some useful for the insights that they provide. Just reading these stories and looking at the lessons that each teaches, or taught me, should start you on your way to creating your own luck. To make your job easier, I have developed a seven-step program that highlights the most important lessons in creating your own luck.

The seven steps are aptitude, attitude, application, acceptance, awareness, abundance, and appreciation. To these basic seven steps I also suggest the three Ps: patience, persistence, and politeness.

Step One—Aptitude

If you are going to create your own luck in business, it is absolutely essential that you have an aptitude for business and for deal making. This does not mean that you are an instinctive dealmaker or that you are born thinking business, business, business. But at a minimum, you do need a basic aptitude for business and a basic enjoyment of the rough and tumble nature of the business world. If you do not have this aptitude for business, you should probably not pursue business at all, as you are unlikely to be able to create your own luck or have any true enjoyment in your business life. This does not mean that you couldn't have a wonderful career as an artist, technician, teacher, or other role as a professional for which you do have a basic aptitude and sense of enjoyment.

Step Two—Attitude

Once you have established that you have an aptitude to pursue some aspect of the business world, develop a positive can-do attitude. Part of your ability to create luck is your belief that you are entitled to unlimited abundance and good fortune. You should cultivate this positive attitude by helping others and focusing on your accomplishments and personal gifts of health, energy, enthusiasm, and willingness to work toward your goals. By cultivating these qualities and acting as if you can take on any problem and contribute to any situation, you will start to see positive results in actually accomplishing these goals. Miraculously, you will begin to cultivate your own ability to be in the right place at the right time and to generally create your own luck.

Step Three—Application

Having a positive attitude and a basic aptitude for the specific area of work you have chosen will get you headed in the right direction, but you still must apply yourself. There is no substitute, particularly at the beginning of an endeavor or a career, for hard work. You need to be focused and ready when opportunity knocks, and you cannot be ready unless you are extremely well prepared in your field of specialization. You need to know the vocabulary of your field and the basic structures and formulas that apply in your industry. You need to apply these principles whenever you can and learn from them so you know, almost intuitively, what is likely to work and what won't, at least based on industry-standard experience. As I have pointed out throughout the book, just applying the principles of the past is never enough, but you can't begin to know when to deviate from the tried and true unless you know what the norms are. In most pursuits, the deviations are not the norm by definition and creating your own luck often will depend upon nothing more than observing trends and knowing what is likely to happen next. I can't emphasize enough, however the importance of applying yourself and obtaining a firm grounding in the fundamentals of your field. Picasso was an extremely accomplished realistic painter before he created modern techniques that defied the norms of art. The same is true for innovators in other fields. Very rarely does it make sense to step up to the plate not knowing what kind of ball is going to be thrown at you or without truly understanding the rules and logistics of the game.

Step Four—Acceptance

Accept yourself as you are—your strengths and weaknesses of personality and character. You will be surprised to learn that no single attribute or quality you possess is ever in and of itself either a strength or weakness. There are always situations in which a quality that is normally a virtue can be a hindrance. Whether a quality is strength or weakness for you depends upon the environment in which you are acting and the specific situation that presents itself to you.

Perhaps you are extremely bright and able to make quick decisions, and you believe that this is your greatest virtue. In most cases it probably is, but there are instances where your superiors do not want a quick decision made, and you risk alienating an entire negotiation by coming up with too facile a solution too easily. You may seem out of place or too ambitious and destroy an opportunity to succeed that a slower-thinking colleague would not risk.

In order to create your own luck you must accept not only your own givens but the vagaries of the business world. You must be willing to accept risk, change, and failure. Someone who never fails is not pushing the envelope far enough and will never reach their full potential. Good luck is less likely to visit the cautious than the brave, and it is only by accepting all that comes before you, even your own fears, that you can move into the space of courage, which will draw good luck to you.

Step Five—Awareness

Heightened self-awareness and awareness of your environment are essential to drawing any good luck to you and realizing that what I call magic is always in the air if you are ready for it and aware of its signs. Having an aptitude, cultivating a positive attitude, applying your skills and knowledge, and accepting yourself and your environment without resistance are keys to heightening your awareness. Anyone who is fully aware can anticipate events and perfect his or her timing and strategy in all deals. Having the right strategy and the right sense of timing automatically improves your odds of success and draws luck to you. There are a number of psychological techniques for increasing your awareness, but perhaps the easiest technique is to simply cultivate your breathing. Some people are born with greater capacity for awareness than others, but anyone can improve their awareness. It is partly a matter of courage. Don't stick your head in the sand and ignore potentially painful or embarrassing situations. It is only by confronting situations head on, for good or bad, and looking clearly at the past, present, and probable future that you will be able to take advantage of silver linings in clouds and miraculously turn lemons into lemonade. Every situation has the potential for profit, or at least self-improvement. If you are aware of your own needs and those of others, you will see and feel the magic that others ignore. They will wonder at your good luck in surviving what on the surface might appear to be disastrous situations or bonehead mistakes. You will know that you created those lucky exits yourself.

Step Six—Abundance

Once you have experienced the five previous steps in a consistent pattern, you will begin to experience the feeling of abundance in your work life. This abundance will probably be manifested by greater earning capacity and a greater inflow of money to you. The key to abundance consciousness, however, is much more fundamental than having additional money. In my own life, having a lot of money in the bank was never as important as having the expectation of receiving a lot of money in the future. In practical terms, I would rather have a hundred thousand dollars rolling in a month with debts of half a million than a million dollars in the bank and no prospects for generating additional revenue. Since the guarantee of future revenues is always subject to some doubt, my abundancy consciousness is more dependent on my self-confidence and belief in my ability to generate future income than actual receivables. This abundance consciousness can be learned and reflects the true nature of reality. There really are, on a universal basis, unlimited resources. You can have everything you want on a material level, and there is a finite limit to what material items you can desire, consume, or appreciate.

At a very basic level, money is merely energy, and the universe contains limitless energy. You need to cultivate an appreciation of the abundance of energy in the universe and your own role in cycling and recycling energy. Even if you have limited money at a particular moment in time, you have limitless enthusiasm, limitless joy, and limitless insights to share with others. By sharing your gifts with others, you restore your own personal store of energy and experience the truly abundant nature of the universe. Once you integrate this abundance consciousness, you will be even more open to the magical good fortune that is trying to reward you every day, if you will only allow it.

Step Seven—Appreciation

Even with a full implementation of the preceding six steps, you will not maximize the good luck in your life unless you also take time out to show and share your appreciation for the good fortune that is yours. Almost all successful entrepreneurs in the later stages of their development show their appreciation of the good fortune that society has bestowed upon them by giving back, whether it be by mentoring others or making billion dollar gifts to the United Nations like Ted Turner. Bill Gates recognizes that his main job today is giving away his fortune, not continuing to double or triple it every year.

It is not enough to show your appreciation at the end of your life. You need to show it every day from the very beginning. You can show it in small ways, including private prayers of thanks, smiles to your employees, words of thanks to colleagues, and sincere gratitude expressed to those who have helped you. There is no person among us who can succeed without a nurturing universe, and we should give thanks whenever possible. Good fortune smiles on those who appreciate their good fortune and who realize that their good fortune is not for their enjoyment alone, but for the betterment of the planet and of others. I believe that anyone who has enjoyed good luck for any length of time would not long continue their string of good luck if they were not consciously appreciative and grateful to the universe for all that they have been given.

In addition to the seven As, the three Ps will help you generate your own good luck. I learned these three Ps many years ago while attending the welcoming address for my sister's class of entering freshman at Smith College in September of 1968. Those were heady times, and President Mendenhall was welcoming one of the last female-only classes in Smith College's distinguished history. His student body was still comprised of almost equal numbers of women who would go on to have business careers and women who would follow what at that time was the more traditional path of marrying and raising children without participating directly in the world of business. Why I was in that audience, I don't really know, other than the logistics of dropping my sister off first before heading for Yale, but his speech left a lasting impression on me, and that has stood me in good stead in business, in life, and in creating good fortune.

Dr. Mendenhall suggested that to succeed at Smith, he would appreciate that the young women remembered the three Ps— patience, politeness, and persistence. Things were changing in the late sixties. My generation wanted the world and we wanted it now! Dr. Mendenhall suggested that we create our world, but more slowly and within the confines of the civilized world as he knew it. He was not willing to guarantee that this would be essential to survive outside of Smith College, but he could guarantee the young women that it would be essential to survive under his reign while they and he were at Smith.

Dr. Mendenhall suggested that in seeking change, politeness be the first rule. More would be gained by suggesting a desire politely than by demanding immediate action. Once a polite request had been made, Dr. Mendenhall recommended persistence. It might not be sufficient to make a single request. There might be several different departments at the college through which a specific request would have to be filtered. He suggested that the young women should be persistent in seeking their goals and that as long as they continued to be polite while being persistent, they were likely to improve their odds of success in achieving their goals.

Being a realist, Dr. Mendenhall also preached patience. He acknowledged that his worldview was not ready to be altered overnight, that some of the requests he was likely to receive were unlikely to meet with his favor. He suggested that the young women be patient with him and his institution. There was perhaps more flexibility and room for compromise than he first imagined on certain issues, but he was equally certain that there were issues on which he would be inflexible. It was best that the young women learn to accept this and be patient in achieving their full desires. They would have opportunities away from Smith College and in later life to exercise their own philosophies and create their own rules, but for the present, he advised patience in those areas in which they would have to endure the status quo.

In my mind, these same qualities, politeness, persistence, and patience will also help you create your own luck. You will minimize negative encounters with others while continuing to focus on your goals and accept life as it is, rather than as you hope it to become. These qualities will enhance your integration of the seven As and facilitate your entry into the land of good luck.

I know that you can achieve greater luck in your daily life by following these guidelines. I am living proof that these principles work, and, with minor modifications, I am sure that they can work for you as well.

CHAPTER 16

THE HIGHEST AND THE BEST

How to Be Your Own Dreamkeeper and Dream Facilitator

Now that you know how to create your own luck, what are you going to do with it? Obviously, you will want to use luck to make your life easier, more productive, more fun, more interesting, and more magical. In the process, you will probably accumulate more money, more possessions, more experiences, and more things. There is nothing wrong with any of those desires or goals, as long as they are balanced.

But fundamentally, you need a goal and a purpose, or there is no point to creating luck in the first place. If you study Abraham Maslow's hierarchy of needs, you will come to agree with his assessment that the more we grow as individuals, the more likely we are to become concerned about others, the notion of community, and the planet as a totality. None of us is alone, and our luck only exists in the context of the rest of humanity. Ultimately, we each have a goal to contribute to improving ourselves and this planet, and, if possible, to leave the world a better place than it was when we entered. This may seem a grandiose assignment, but it isn't. To improve the planet, it is only necessary that each individual strive to be the best person possible and to help others be their best as well.

To a large extent, the same principles that apply to making great business deals also apply to making a concerted effort to saving the planet. In the deepest sense, the ultimate way of being the deal is dealing with the planet and the higher purpose for which we were all born. I personally find the mere improvement of living conditions, increased efficiency, and greater opportunities for individuals to concentrate on creativity, joy, humor, art, sport, nature, and achievement is satisfaction enough. Others have told me that they seek a deeper evolution for themselves to evolve spiritually to be their highest selves. Either way, either direction, both the inner search and the outer expression of goodness complement our human purpose and contribute directly to improving the planet and leaving it in the best shape possible for those who will come after us.

This is a book about deal making in the context of business and money. As a member of the sixties generation, I was part of the generation that rejected the mindless affluence of the fifties and criticized the pursuit of money. I remember distinctly telling my mother that I did not think that I would bother to get a college degree, but instead just take courses that interested me. She warned me that this would be foolish. I asked her why, and she said, "Well, without a degree, you won't get as good a job, and you won't make as much money." "Why do I need money?" I asked. "Well, if you don't have any money, you won't have any power in this society." "Why will I want to have power?" I asked. "You will come to understand that you will want power. Without power, you cannot choose your life course or align with your deeper purpose," she concluded.

At the time, I thought that I would be different, that my generation would find a new way, would create a new system of politics and economics. On the surface, I was wrong, and yet I know from associating with members of that generation who have now accumulated great wealth and power that despite the outer-seeming sellout of our earlier ideals, many of us are consciously working to create the utopia on earth that we envisioned as adolescent men and women in the sex, drugs, and rock-and-roll era in which we became adults.

We do this within the context of business and money. We believe that money is an energy that can help us achieve our goals. We are careful not to become too attached to the objects that money can buy, but instead become attached to the limitless consciousness of abundance and power that generating money can give us. There is a level on which many of us are still revolutionaries participating in the system, just as our parents did, but with our own subversive agendas to radically and forever create a system both economic and political that is more in touch with the true needs of the planet, the individual, and our communities.

I have spent much of the last forty years exploring and benefiting from the breakthroughs in computer technology. The technology is marvelous in and of itself on an intellectual level, and it's exciting to contemplate and to create with, yet we are more aware than ever that technology itself is neutral. It is only through committed effort that technology will ever actually solve the true problems of humanity, or contribute to making the world a better place for all of us.

One of the concepts that has governed much of my business life is the concept of the Highest and the Best. My first familiarity with this term came in relation to real estate transactions. It was pointed out to me that a building would have greater value for its owner if the building were used to its highest and best purpose. For example, since commercially zoned buildings can garner higher rents than private residences, it is not the highest and best use of a commercial piece of property to use it as a personal residence. You may choose to do this for personal reasons, but from the pure economic perspective, you would not be making the highest and best use of your land.

When clients come to me with projects, I look at their goals in terms of the highest and best use of their talents. It may be more interesting to a particular client to write a book on an esoteric piece of software that might sell only ten thousand copies, but if that author is talented enough to write on a topic that could reach millions, I suggest that he or she consider that opportunity first. In most cases, clients want to balance their need to make money with their hobbies and interests. Many times the projects that can make the most money are just as interesting as those that would not be economically viable.

On a higher plane, each one of us has a highest and best destiny. I consciously try to help my clients at least in regards to their work life to achieve this highest and best destiny. I try to apply this same rule to myself, and it is never easy. It requires a constant willingness to remake myself, to push my limits, and to explore unchartered territory. It is demanding, but for me it is also the source of my personal creativity, without which life would become dull, predictable, and less vibrant.

Over time, I have been so consistent with holding this perspective with people I meet for the first time that they sometimes wonder how I can cut right to the heart of their goals. I became so used to thinking of myself as the keeper of the dreams for my writer clients that I wrote a poem entitled "Dreamkeeper."

In this moment
I am the dreamkeeper
I have come to awaken your dream

I am the dreamkeeper
awaken me to your highest dream

My gift to you
I can no longer deny
In your passion
I grant you everything

I return to you again and again
the sun, the stars from which all began

In this moment
I am the dreamkeeper

I have come to awaken your dream
I am the dreamkeeper
Awaken me to your highest dream
We can jump into a time machine
and set it ahead or behind
we can live one moment of eternity
in just a minute of time.

I am the dreamkeeper
I have come to awaken your dream
I am the dreamkeeper
Awaken me to your highest dream.

We all have the capacity to be dreamkeepers, keepers of our own dreams and facilitators of the dreams of others. We think that our dreams are private individual fantasies, but in reality, they can be collective collaborations. The best dreams require interaction with the rest of humanity. I hope that you will use your good luck to awaken yourself and those you care most deeply about to your own highest and best dream, and I also hope that you serve as a catalyst for pragmatic, business-oriented dreamers everywhere.